YOU and

the WORLD

TO COME

BOOKS BY MAXWELL DROKE

YOU AND THE WORLD TO COME

THE SPEAKER'S HANDBOOK OF HUMOR

GOODBYE TO G.I.

PEOPLE: HOW TO GET THEM TO DO
WHAT YOU WANT THEM TO DO

MAKING A SUCCESS OF SALESMANSHIP

ANTHOLOGY OF ANECDOTES

STAG LINES: THE ANTHOLOGY OF
VIRILE VERSE

YOU

HARPER & BROTHERS

Publishers NEW YORK

and the WORLD

TO COME

by Maxwell Droke

To the Younger Generation:
Ever Our Inspiration

CONTENTS

FOREWORD

A Few Words about the Book . . .

and the Man Who Wrote It

SOME READERS may wonder why Maxwell Droke, well known as a writer of humor for leading American magazines and a compiler of books of comic stories and witticisms, has written a "serious" book. Serious books, such persons may think, should be written by serious people. Have we here a clown who is trying to play Hamlet?

Of course Maxwell Droke is not a clown, or not all the time. But, if he were, that would be no disqualification for making some shrewd guesses about the future of mankind. I, for one, have a high respect for clowns. There is a world of difference between professional fools, of whom we have all too few, and amateur fools, of whom we have all too many. The wisest characters in Shakespeare's tragedies are his clowns and fools, and if his kings had taken their advice they would have been alive at the end of the fifth act.

As for tragedy, it was Horace Walpole who said, "The world is a comedy to those who think, a tragedy to those who feel." There is something intellectual, rational, analytical about the person who detects, and especially the person who writes about, the comic aspects of life. Such a person is likely to be clear-eyed, unemotional, not easily dismayed. So, since Maxwell Droke for many years has been a writer and collector of humor, he may have a sharper mind and a sharper pen for the present task than the ponderous pundit.

It is easy to be typed as a certain kind of writer. This is nothing new. Sir Walter Scott realized this when, for a change of pace, he left the novels of Scotland which had made him famous and wrote of medieval England in *Ivanhoe*. In the preface to that book he said: "The public are, in general, very ready to adopt the opinion that he who has pleased them in one peculiar mode of composition is, by means of that very talent, rendered incapable of venturing upon other subjects." Denying this to be the case, he added: "The same capacity which carries a man to popularity in one department will obtain for him success in another." And Scott, turning abruptly to a new field, produced his most popular book and proved his point.

But Maxwell Droke does not need to convince us, with the present book, that he can write seriously as well as playfully. He has already done this many times over. For out in Indianapolis he has built up a very successful publishing business, and in *Quote,* the weekly digest he has issued for twenty years, he has developed a unique magazine of wide influence.

Nor is this Droke's first venture into the writing of books that aim to do more than merely entertain. The long list of these, over a period of many years, includes *Making a Success of Salesmanship, People: How to Get Them to Do What You Want Them to Do* and his manual for returning World War II veterans, *Goodbye to G.I.,* which was recommended by the Book-of-the-Month Club.

After all, writers of humor are essentially serious people. More than usually observant and lively minded, they are also more than usually concerned about at least the minor frailties of human nature. The major vices they may be inclined to leave to the preachers, the philosophers, and the police. Their subject is people, and they examine people pretty closely in search of imperfections and the ridiculous. But, unless they are bitter satirists, they have a real affection for the human race (made all the more interesting by its foibles) and hope for its ultimate improvement.

So it is that perhaps precisely the right person to look into the future of our children, the kind of lives they will lead on this planet (as well, possibly, as nearby ones), is a man like Maxwell Droke, whose experience with humor will help rather than handicap him.

Add to this the fabulously wide reading and pack-rat way of collecting facts required by editing *Quote*. Add also a knack for being lucid and entertaining on subjects that could very well be dull. Who, then, could do it better?

Now settle down for an informative, exciting, and delightful look at Tomorrow.

RICHARD ARMOUR

(Richard Armour, a Harvard Ph.D. and Professor of English at Scripps College, whose nineteen books include both scholarly works and popular humor and satire, is himself an example of the double career he describes.)

PREFACE

"—And Ever Shall Be"

SOME YEARS AGO I went to San
Francisco to address a group of insurance executives on the subject
of our economic future. As plane-reading I took along a novel by a
young Frenchman writing under the nom de plume of Vercors. The
story concerned a group of scientists who suddenly came upon a
colony of animals more closely resembling the human species than
any yet known. The question, argued for sixty thousand words, was
simply this: Were those creatures primitive men or advanced animals?

Well, I recall suggesting to my insurance group that the decision
could have been reached in ten minutes, and related in ten pages.
It should have been necessary only to toss a crystal ball into their
midst. If they regarded it merely as a bright bauble, they could be
only animals. But if they began peering into it and asking questions,
we'd have to classify them with the men. For only man has a "tomorrow" mind. He alone of the living kingdom is possessed of a yen to
look around corners.

In writing the present volume, however, I have been scrupulously
careful to stay away from any suggestion of magic, black or otherwise. In no instance have I leaned upon necromancy or fortunetelling. I have no psychic sense or mystic powers. It would be difficult
to find in the space of a day's jet journey anyone with a lower
intuitive perception. These surmises on the future—and I have made

them rather freely—are based in all instances on deductions from clearly discernible trends. It is simply a case of judging the future by the past and by the direction in which we continue to travel.

In 1953, in England, Sir Charles Galton Darwin, grandson of the great biologist, published a small book called *The Next Million Years*. Two years later Sir George Thomson, the Nobel prize-winning physicist wrote a similarly comprehensive work called *The Foreseeable Future*.

I have envied these men their broader canvas. For it always Is easier to foretell the future the farther you remove yourself from it. Our sociologists and men of science know a great number of things that in all probability will come to pass within a hundred years. And an infinitely greater number that may be spaced, say, within a thousand years.

But when it comes down to drawing a fine bead on, let us say, the few years that remain to us of the twentieth century, the problem becomes incredibly complex. So, if I have been in spots a bit hazy as to precise dates I beg your indulgence.

I wish to take this opportunity to express my gratitude to the human race. Wherever an illustrative example has been required, some member of this group has stepped forward to volunteer. Without this invaluable aid the work would have been far more complex. And much less rewarding.

MAXWELL DROKE

YOU and

the WORLD

TO COME

I THE WORLD THAT WAS

HARRY . . .

Pierre phoned that he would take me for my permanent at four o'clock. I'll go on from there with Helen to the P.T.A. meeting. There's a tv dinner and salad stuff in the refrigerator. Get yourself some strawberries or ice cream from the deep freeze.

Ralph will be in on the 8:15 flight. He will take a taxi, so you needn't go to the airport.

We are going in Helen's car; mine is low on gas. Please be a dear and take it to the filling station for me.

I should be home a little after nine.

LUCILLE

This note, perfectly intelligible and perhaps even a bit reminiscent to an average householder in suburbia, was written by the wife of one of my associates. And written, I may add, without the slightest thought that she was producing an item of considerable Social Significance.

The message came into my hands when the lady's husband apologetically scribbled a memo on the reverse side—it was the only scrap of paper he had in his pocket at the moment. I was about to discard this historic document when, on an illuminating intuitive hunch, I turned to it for closer study.

The remarkable thing about this hastily written directive— mundane and matter-of-fact as it admittedly is—is that nearly all of the references share a common distinction. The permanent wave, the Parent-Teacher Association, the term "tv," the electric refrigerator, the deep freeze, the airplane, the airport, the taxi cab, and the filling station all are developments of our twentieth century. Only the telephone and the automobile, which play supporting roles, were known in 1900. The telephone was hardly an accepted household necessity before 1910. The automobile remained a rich man's plaything until after the First World War.[1]

I was within a week of my fourth birthday when the twentieth century dawned. We grew up together in a world which most of you who read these pages would find a strange and alien adventure.

At the time I was born my father was a Methodist minister in Chattanooga, Tennessee. Soon after the turn of the century he accepted the presidency of a university in Kansas—one of the many small religious schools then flourishing. (This, incidentally, was the school at which, in an earlier period, President Eisenhower's parents had met as students. I am told that they courted on the university campus.)

Born in a border state, of parents divided in their allegiance between the North and the South, I grew up in the West, and

[1] To forestall an avalanche of correspondence let it be stated the author is fully aware that 2,000 women gathered in Washington on February 27, 1897, to organize the National Congress of Mothers, and that the gathering was the forerunner of today's Parent-Teacher Association. However, neither the term "P.T.A." nor its national significance developed until well into the twentieth century.

in my capacity as an usher at the Opera House in our town I contrived to see *East Lynne* three times. It was a background hardly lacking in variety.

My father, because of his considerable renown as a fund raiser, enjoyed a salary rather larger than the common emolument of educators. (The Endowment Fund was then, as now, a vitally important factor.) My mother was a writer of juvenile fiction and in later years a Lyceum and Chautauqua artist, giving "readings" from her own and other works. My older sister was a librarian.

I mention these points to emphasize that ours was not an underprivileged household. We were in what at that period was termed "comfortable circumstances." Our lack of presently termed common necessities was a lack shared by all of our friends. We didn't even realize there *was* a lack. The pinch of privation is experienced only when you have higher standards for comparison. We lived as well as anyone in our community. And that, we felt, was rather high on the hog.

There were five of us children—a moderate-sized family for the period. We lived in a fairly large house, owned by the university, in one of the better neighborhoods. There was a front parlor (my older sister insisted on calling it a "drawing room," which rather puzzled us youngsters since no kid would have been permitted to enter that rarefied area equipped with even a harmless slate pencil).

The parlor was elegantly furnished with a sofa and chairs upholstered in a rather startling blue. There was a huge boxlike mahogany piano, too (later traded for a more stylish upright). A couple of small tables ("taborets" in the lexicon of my senior sibling) held potted plants. Some enlarged family portraits, elaborately framed, and a couple of oil paintings executed by my Aunt Eunice completed the plenishings, except for the Family Bible and a plush-covered photograph album which reposed, with a vase of wax flowers, on a mahogany center table.

There was a library, too, which my father used as a sort of auxiliary office and where he received official visitors.

But—there was no bathroom! Indeed, for at least the first decade of the century there wasn't a bathroom in the entire community. In our household the family bathed in turn on Saturday afternoons in a galvanized washtub set in the middle of the kitchen floor. Water for these ablutions was heated on a coal-burning kitchen range (a kerosene cookstove in summer). Each child was supposed to empty his tub and fill it for the next in line.

I had seen bathrooms, of course, stopping with my parents at hotels in Topeka and Kansas City, but I am quite sure it never occurred to me that they were to be found in ordinary homes.

The two-bathroom house was, of course, a much later development. My older brother, who worked for George W. Vanderbilt, used to tell an amusing story of that period when the financier was enamored of the North Carolina mountain country. Vanderbilt once decided to build a hunting lodge in a remote fastness of the Blue Ridge—a modest little log cabin of a dozen rooms or so. He gave the assignment to a local contractor. Returning a month later he was quite annoyed to find nothing had been done.

"Can't make a move," said the contractor testily. "Them plans is wrong."

Mr. Vanderbilt replied that the plans had been drawn up by a New York architectural firm in which he had considerable confidence.

"Can't he'p it," persisted the contractor. "They is all wrong. Why, Mr. Vanda'bilt," he concluded, "if I was to go ahead and build that place accordin' to them plans, you'd wind up havin' yose'f a house with *two* bathrooms!"

There is a tradition that turn-of-the-century families lived in gastronomical abundance. Tales of the "groaning board" have persisted, and can be pretty well substantiated. Housewives prided themselves on "setting a good table." In the summer months, at least, we had considerable variety, for every household had its own half-acre garden patch. Fruits and berries were plentiful.

One little-recognized reason for the variety of offerings was that, in the smaller communities at least, there was little refrigeration. (We had an icebox, dating from about 1903 or 1904; most of our neighbors lacked this luxury and bought ice only for an occasional freezer of homemade ice cream.) The common practice was to cook up everything available for dinner (the big midday meal), then warm up and perhaps supplement the leftovers for supper.

From the time of the first frost in the fall until the arrival of early "garden truck" in the spring our daily diet would hardly have intrigued the average person of today.

There were no out-of-season vegetables—no lettuce or other greens for salads, and no fresh fruits. In the long, bleak period from September until May or June our breakfast fruits were alternately prunes, dried peaches and dried apricots. Bananas, it seems to me, were available most of the time, but they were not commonly considered an item of staple diet. The only time I recall eating them was on train trips. We usually bought a few to "piece out" our shoe-box lunches brought from home. Sometime between Thanksgiving and Christmas the grocers would each import a crate of oranges "for the holiday trade." Each child could expect one in his Christmas stocking, which he would treasure for days before the elaborate ritual of peeling and eating. And there would be three or four oranges left over for the making of "ambrosia." This was a delicacy to be expected only at Christmastime. It consisted of sliced and diced oranges with a liberal sprinkling of shredded coconut.

All in all, I hardly think you'd care to trade your frozen foods, imported delicacies, excellent meats, and varied desserts for the choicest turn-of-the-century fare. It may seem rather sumptuous, viewed from a distance, but most of the time it was pretty dull.

On Saturday mornings there were chores to be done before we could turn our thoughts to play. Cleaning lamp chimneys and polishing shoes are routine tasks that stand out in recollection. In summer all children—boys and girls alike—went barefoot. The big picnic on the last day of school was traditionally a time to cast aside shoes and stockings. Except for Sunday-school attendance, they would not be donned again until the first day of a new school term. This was a boon which we anticipated for weeks: an adventure in freedom mitigated only by a few stone bruises, an occasional bee sting, and the nightly foot-washing ordeal at the cistern pump.

In summer, too, most small boys had their hair clipped as close as possible, presenting an effect rather like that of a host of juvenile Yul Brynners. But no one was concerned about appearance. Not only was the effect delightfully cool, but there was no bothersome brushing. And parents were not unmindful of the fact that their closely shorn brood would require fewer twenty-five cent haircuts during the season.

Of course we rather missed those periodic visits to the U-R Next Barber Shop. It was the only place we could encounter the *Police Gazette*. We turned to it with complete fascination, oblivious of the sinister implications. The barbershop, too, was a spot where cigarettes were bootlegged (Kansas having at that time a statute against their open sale), but we were quite unconscious of such devious dealings.

It was fun, too, to check over the rows of individual shaving mugs, set aside for the exclusive use of just about every important man in town. Pop's was there, in the center of the third row. But he rarely patronized a tonsorial parlor. He wore no beard —which was rather unusual for the period—and rather prided himself on his dexterity with an old-fashioned straight razor. I once observed him, seated in the men's room of a railroad station, shave himself perfectly without the aid of a mirror.

Now that I come to think of it, the ladies of the period were somewhat slighted. I suppose there were beauty parlors of a sort in Kansas City—there must have been, for it was a wild and raucous metropolis in those days with money flowing freely. But we hadn't even so much as a local hairdresser.

My sister had an esoteric collection of bottles and boxes on her dressing table, but I doubt that rouge was included in the early years of the century. Rouge was "paint" and "painted ladies" were beyond the pale.

But in those early 1900's there was among the feminine contingent an unmistakable undercurrent of—well, not exactly rebellion, but a restless dissatisfaction with status. The young state of Wyoming had given women the vote in 1890. There was a good deal of talk about that. Generally the belief in our Middle-western world seemed to be that if women wanted the vote—and they obviously did—they were pretty sure to get it. And maybe it wouldn't be such a bad move after all. Mother was a sort of intellectual supporter of this movement. I don't suppose she ever attended a feminist meeting—and certainly never marched in a parade. But she talked a good game.

The reform in feminine apparel had already begun by the very early 1900's; the long, dust-catching ruffles had been abandoned for more modish—and certainly more sensible—ankle-length skirts.

I recall one hot summer afternoon, about 1902 or 1903. Mother was entertaining the ladies of the faculty. We children, as usual, had been banished to the back yard. Normally there were few things that interested us less than adult conversation. But the act of forcible eviction piqued our curiosity. So we sent my younger brother, via a circuitous route, to creep beneath the open window, listen and report. He came back in due course to tell us that the ladies were discussing the relative merits of wearing one petticoat versus two.

I don't recall just when electricity came into general use in our community. But in 1908 my older brother imported the first vacuum cleaner our town had ever seen. Certainly at that time electricity was not widely used, for this contrivance operated with a hand pump. With my older brother running the hose, my younger brother and I alternated at the pump. We set up a housecleaning service that proved sensationally successful. That spring and summer we must have cleaned practically every rug and carpet in town, thus winning the gratitude of the masculine element who had previously been obliged to do the rug-beating. We ran into only one complication: This newfangled device drew out so much dirt that women refused to credit their eyes. We soon learned to show them the empty dust receptacle before starting our operations. At the fantastic charge of one dollar an hour (for the three of us) we must have made more money during those months than the local bank cashier.

It was rather late in the first decade of the century that we began to notice a subtle change in our situation. Our social status remained unimpaired, but we were increasingly conscious of the fact that we were not sharing fully in the growing prosperity of the period. The educators, the ministers, and others in the "cultural" group had to face the fact that their more or less fixed incomes were not keeping pace with the steadily rising cost of living. Almost imperceptibly we were becoming first-class citizens with second-class purchasing power.

More and more of our friends and neighbors were acquiring prized possessions clearly beyond our reach—shiny, sputtering automobiles, the new "mission" furniture, some of the early electric appliances, fur scarves and muffs. And, of course, the teen-agers of the time were beginning to turn to mechanical music—Edison's great invention, the phonograph, with its huge morning-glory horn and cylinder records—ballads by Ada Jones and Billy Murray, and such side-splitting monologues as *Cohen on the Telephone.*

Recreations grew a bit more sophisticated. Croquet lost some of its lure when tennis was introduced on the university campus. There was even some vague talk of converting the sizable acreage known as "Rafter's pasture" into a golf course, but the Chautauqua interests held prior rights. This was the site of their summer encampment and they refused to give ground.

Some of the more daring "sports" were by now taking their Saturday evening "dates" to the local hostelry where an elegant table d'hôte dinner was served for seventy-five cents—including oysters in the R months. There was a player piano—a marvelous new invention—in one of the back parlors. Rumor had it that some of the couples indulged in dancing. A girl who accepted these "hotel dates" was considered a little "fast" and probably would not be asked to sing in one of the church choirs—unless she had an exceptionally fine voice.

To most of us youngsters "vacation" was primarily a period when you didn't have to go to school. We had time for play, to be sure. But we also worked as a matter of course at whatever odd jobs we could turn up—mowing lawns, tending gardens, picking fruits and berries. I worked as often as I could in the job printing department of the *Signal,* our Democratic weekly in a strong Republican community. (The *Signal* captured the school printing contract one year and I ran my own fifth-grade report card on a small hand-fed press.) The lure of printer's ink was so impelling I would have worked for nothing. But Frank Jarrell was not strongly intuitive in such matters. He paid me ten cents an hour.

I am a little vague as to just when the idea of summer "vacation trips" began to evolve as a fixed pattern in our community. Two or three families attended the World's Fair in St. Louis in 1904, and I recall at least one group setting off for the Jamestown Exposition in 1907. But it probably was 1910 or a little later before any considerable number began, as a regular practice, setting aside two or three weeks for an excursion to the Chicago Stock Yards, Niagara Falls, or Yellowstone National Park. It was about this time, too, that some of the well-to-do farmers began tripping to California for a few weeks in the dead of winter.

All these developments were symptomatic of a prosperity which we, somehow, failed to share. Everybody else seemed to be doing well, although naturally the farmers suffered in a "drought year"—and this meant bad business for the merchants as well. (When heavy thunderstorms broke a prolonged drought in the summer of 1902, the dignified merchants of Topeka cast off their shoes and socks, rolled up their trousers, and waded joyously in the flooded gutters. For them it was literally a rain of gold.)

Small industry was beginning to flourish in the Midwest by 1910 and the skilled artisans were coming up rapidly from the rear. It was the daughter of a brickmason, I recall, who wore the first evening gown I ever beheld. She wore it ("tastelessly," the other females sniffed) to a performance of the Swiss Bell Ringers, one of the Lyceum attractions held in the university auditorium.

Well, that was the evolving pattern. Soon we were in the midst of World War I, that era of madcap memories when American industry performed miracles with routine rhythm, and in the process turned values topsy-turvy. It was during this period that the fixed-income group fell hopelessly behind the procession. They have never since made much of a recovery.

Then came the teeming twenties—the era of Flaming Youth. Mothers who had considered a drugstore root beer a mildly daring adventure, and who had blushed to reveal a well-turned ankle as they were helped into and out of buggies, had daughters who swigged illicit gin from flashy flasks and bounced into Stutz Bear Cats with the nonchalance (and nudity) of a nymph.

But now the plot becomes faintly familiar. This is about where you came in. Personal reminiscences and reflections will suffice to fill in the gaps. So, let us move on to our consideration of The World That Is to Be.

II THE WORLD TO BE

WHEN I SAY, as I often must in group discussions, that our next generation will live in a collectivist social order, the consternation and apprehension of parents is at once obvious.

To those who dissent from this judgment, I have one stock response: "Why do you anticipate a change?"

The simple truth is that we are living in a collectivist society right now. More than half of our people have never known any other order. We shall continue to live in this fashion for the foreseeable future—relying chiefly upon organized groups to determine our social and economic destiny—because we like it that way. Nowhere in the offing is there a hint of any consequential opposition.

Yes, we are collectivists. And we may anticipate more and more collective action in the years that lie ahead. The group will increasingly insulate the individual from the disasters and defeats, the hazards and handicaps of daily life. He is assured, if not smooth sailing, at least freedom from complete submersion. He may flounder, but he won't founder.

Significantly, no Congress in a quarter of a century has made the slightest attempt to rescind any of the early social legislation inspired by Franklin D. Roosevelt; no administration has sug-

gested such a course. Because, in the final analysis, no one really
wants to surrender Social Security, Unemployment Compensation, Low-Cost Housing, and the sundry other benefits that have
accrued to us through the years.

Obviously the economic plight of the country in the early
1930's spurred many of our social reforms and assured a minimum of opposition to their passage. But in any case they could
not have been long deferred. We had been inching our way
toward collectivist action almost from the turn of the century.

In the thirty years between the administrations of the two
crusading Roosevelts we observed passage of the Pure Food and
Drug Act to prohibit the misbranding and adulteration of our
daily fare; the establishment of the Children's Bureau in the
Department of Commerce and Labor; passage of the Keating-
Owen Act barring from interstate commerce products of child
labor; passage (with federal blessing) of state laws regulating the
ages, wages and hours of working children; adoption (under
President Hoover) of the annual White House Conference on
Child Health and Protection; the establishment of the Federal
Reserve System as a banking reform measure; the Federal Trade
Commission providing machinery for the regulation of corpora-
tions in interstate commerce; the Federal Farm Loan Act setting
up Farm Loan Banks throughout the nation.

During this period we voted (and twice increased) pensions
for veterans of the Mexican and Civil wars; adopted the
Soldiers' Bonus Bill providing twenty-year endowment insurance
for veterans of World War I; repeatedly enlarged the ranks of
civil service; extended, as early as 1912, the eight-hour day to
all federal employees, and as a final gesture of the presumably
"conservative" period we passed the Boulder Dam Project Act
committing the United States government to participation in the
production of hydroelectric power.

All these actions predated—most of them by many years—
the New Deal era. They are, in one way or another, group move-

ments to isolate the individual from exploitation; to guard his health and happiness; protect his pocketbook and assure his well-being. But at the time few would have cared—or dared—to suggest that they marked a developing trend toward a collective social order.

"Collectivist" was a term vaguely associated with those long-haired, wild-eyed Socialists, and, later, with that emerging philosophy of the Slavic mind known as "Communism."

Parenthetically it may be said that the Russian corruption of Communism is the supreme irony of our age. Communism, in its essence, is one of the noblest concepts that ever emanated from the mind of man. Of course it has a fatal weakness: it will work only in an aggregation of angels. But it has nevertheless been the dream of idealists from Plato and Sir Thomas More to Bronson Alcott and Upton Sinclair.

But the Bolsheviks came along and put an end to all that. They wrapped a few thin shreds of Communism about their military machine, flaunted the banner of atheism, and in forty short years made the vision of centuries forever repugnant to the Western mind.

Obviously "collectivist" as we use the term here doesn't imply anything remotely resembling Soviet Communism. I think you need not be unduly apprehensive that the coming generation will embrace a Communist philosophy. They should, if anything, be more repelled by it than their elders are today. Communism can no longer trade, as it has in our generation, on its novelty, its mystery, its promise of sweeping revolutionary changes in the economic structure. After forty years of futile experimentation, Russian Communists have done very little to improve the lot of the common man. Certainly there is nothing in the record to date to fire the imagination or arouse the envy of dissident Americans.

And dissident Americans, it would seem, are a vanishing species. There is no "downtrodden" group in this country; no submerged faction with the slightest prospect of anything to gain

from revolutionary action. The humblest American already has
infinitely more than Communism can offer. And with the modern
world's improved communication system, he is well aware of
that fact.

Of course there are healthy gripes and growls, as there should
be in any democratic country where a citizen is permitted to
voice his vexation against pinprick irritations. Here and there
an individual may be annoyed because there is no parking space
when he stops by to pick up his monthly unemployment compensation check. Or another, whose prosperity is directly affected
by the spending proclivities of our multiplied millions of women
wage earners, may thoughtlessly urge that all females be banished
to the washtubs, the vacuum cleaners and the nurseries.

But these are amateur jeremiads, mere practice plaints put
forth to keep the channels of remonstration free of rust. We are
pretty happy with things the way they are—and the way they
promise to be as far as we can see into the future.

Whether the social system that is now evolving—and which
our children will more fully develop—is "socialistic" must depend, I suppose, on your definition. Certainly some of the legislation of our time, looking toward the more equitable distribution
of wealth, would have been viewed by our turn-of-the-century
parents as wildly socialistic. Yet we have not given up, nor does
there appear to be any prospect that we shall renounce, the
capitalistic system with its varying rewards for achievements
under the banner of free enterprise.

What we have undertaken in one generation—and must bring
to full fruition in the next—is a program guaranteeing every
citizen decent minimum emoluments, without at the same time
setting any limit on his maximum achievements or rewards, ex-
cepting only such restrictions as are imposed by an expanding
Internal Revenue System.

This objective of security for the individual is a very old
dream in the world, but only in the West is it being attained

within the framework of a republican form of government. Only
here is a citizen assured the essentials of roof, raiment and rations
without ideological surrender. He can believe anything he
chooses—and he chooses to believe that he is a most fortunate
fellow.

There are, it has seemed to me, four factors in this country
tending to shape a standardized, prefabricated social structure
which probably will endure in its essentials for the remainder of
our century.

The first of these factors, as we have seen, is a paternal government, endeavoring in all sincerity, and with the best of intentions,
to banish poverty and privation; to give the individual, for the
first time in human history, a realistic measure of social security.
Here is a security that extends quite literally from the womb to
the tomb, embracing the health and welfare of a household, as
well as assuring its economic stability.

A second factor is the corporate employer who, in half a
century, has changed characterization from mean malefactor to
nice old nanny.

In the early years of this century the great American corporations still were memorials to the man who had built them—such
powerful industrialists as Andrew Carnegie, John D. Rockefeller
and Henry Ford. Generally speaking they reflected the philosophies of these men and did not always take into account
corporate responsibility to the individual.

The modern corporation with its multiple ownership is run
by "hired hands" who have been quick to sense the value of sound
employee relations.

A good deal has been written of late concerning the junior
corporation executive, a type that has come to be known as "the
organization man." We have seen how the corporation, sensing
the value of these pawns, has provided an ever-increasing variety
of protective services in their behalf. There are pensions and

profit-sharing plans; health and accident insurance programs; home loans; savings proposals, and so on down the line.

The significant point, however, is that these corporate overtures are no longer extended exclusively to the executives. They are now, in most organizations, equally available to the senior vice-president and the newest filing clerk. The two related reasons for these gestures are to inspire a higher degree of corporate loyalty and to reduce employee turnover, which has become increasingly a business bugaboo.

There is considerable competition among corporations, especially in communities where labor is at a premium, to devise new services appealing to a prospective employee.

One large pharmaceutical house of my acquaintance, in addition to offering the customary recreational facilities, has set up evening extension classes in a variety of subjects including art, photography and public speaking. Capable instructors are brought in to conduct the classes. The company picks up the check.

"Picking up the check" is indeed a rather general practice with corporations these days in their employee relations programs. Even in such items as health and accident insurance, the company may absorb a portion of the premium. And in virtually all cases where an employee buys company stock the corporation has some form of matching procedure.

But of course the employee does have his share to pay. In most offices the list of items to be deducted from a worker's pay is growing steadily. These "holdouts" include specified sums for income tax reserve and social security, plus obligations the individual may have voluntarily assumed for the purchase of savings bonds, group insurance, company stock, etc. Finally, in some areas, there may be deductions for pledges to the community fund, Red Cross, and other charitable and civic organizations.

"The modern corporation," said a recent observer, "is not only our source of livelihood; it is becoming the guardian of our lives as well. To any average employee in an average city 'the company' is likely to serve as physician, lawyer, banker, investment counsel, insurance agent, recreational adviser and community conscience."

There is a classic story of a chap who, through some failure of the automatic machinery to function, received a check with his name properly inscribed, but otherwise blank. "Just as I thought," he mused, "my deductions have finally caught up with my salary!"

It may be argued that these protective practices apply only to the very large corporations and thus affect a relatively small segment of the total work force.

To that contention there are two answers: First, the "very large corporations" are steadily increasing in number, in size and in scope; their production plants and branches are spreading everywhere. A second point is that wherever and whenever "the big boys" move into a community the effect on labor relations is immediate and revolutionary. To compete for the more desirable office and factory workers, the smaller employers must offer their own special inducements. They cannot always match the big-time profit-sharing and pension plans. But they can, and often must, increase their hourly rates, spruce up their rest rooms, and present ingenious new recreational inducements.

Such social gains as the five-day week, the paid vacation and the coffee break—now virtually universal in American business —can be credited to the permeating influence of the corporate employer.

And it is interesting to note in passing that the influence of the corporate employer is extending well beyond the business realm. An instance may be cited in the many colleges and universities that now offer personnel programs comparable to the best in industry.

I had recent occasion to talk with a professor whose university was a pioneer in providing "benefits." I knew that he had origi-

nally opposed the move, but I found him, after two years of
experience, somewhat mollified. "I still think it is humiliating
and debilitating to the intelligent adult to have an IBM machine
for a nursemaid," he asserted, "but there are advantages that
can't be laughed away.

"For the first time in my academic life I am standing on a
firm foundation. My future is assured. A pension plan will take
care of me at retirement age. If my health fails, or if I die in
the interval, the university-sponsored insurance will provide for
my family. At stated intervals the university buys a savings bond
for me and tucks it away in the professional piggy bank. I never
see these government debentures, but I know they're there—and
they represent the first systematic savings plan I've ever had.

"Do you know," he concluded, "I hate to admit it, but I
really believe that most of us on the faculty would be better off
if the school would carry this idea even further; if, in addition
to what they are doing now, they'd provide us with a house, an
automobile, take over our other fixed obligations, and give us
each a few thousand dollars a year for routine expenses . . .
Well, who knows, it may come to that someday!"

A third factor making its contribution toward a pattern of
social conformity is the labor union. We readily recognize the
familiar figure of the union leader, ever ready to battle for the
maximum wage with a fringe on top. But the forces of organized
labor have other and more subtle missions to perform. One of
these tasks is to educate the membership in the realities of
political life, so that they may present a united front at the polls.
The "labor record" of each candidate is analyzed and evaluated.
The union member is told how to mark his ballot and, spiritually
at least, is shepherded into the voting booth.

Though it never loses sight of material objectives, the union
has been active in these late years in obtaining social benefits
for its membership. Not always has the corporate employer given
gladly to lighten the lot of the lowly worker. Sometimes these

gains have been attained only as a consequence of a joint meeting of labor and management, with labor holding the lead joint in a striking position.

A union admittedly performs many services for the worker which, in an earlier day, would have been considered the obligation—and the privilege—of an individual to do for himself. The United Auto Workers, for example, now has a special department to counsel and guide older and retired workers.

Finally, let us consider our fourth contributing factor—the associations. These may be trade, professional or craft groups; they may be comprised of lawyers, doctors, merchants or chiefs of police. But collectively they have done a great deal to standardize the behavior not only of those within the group but of outsiders as well. Granting that these group efforts have generally been "for the good of the order" and tending on the whole toward a more ethical and seemly conduct of business or profession, the fact remains that in yet another area the individual has become submissive to the group; once again the vestments have been cut to the pattern of conformity.

I suggest at this point the quite apparent fact that your children are more likely to work for some branch of government or for a corporate structure than to adventure as individual entrepreneurs. At the turn of this century three workers in five were self-employed. Now the percentage has been reversed; at least three in five are working for others. In another twenty-five years the self-employed person will be a rarity in our social system.

Even now, it may be pointed out, the man who owns and operates his own business has only four chances in ten of earning as much as the man who elects to accept a supervisory position in business. I shall not be surprised to see that ratio lowered in the next decade.

Of course this doesn't mean that we shall lack our entrepreneurs. Some types of enterprise always will call for individual ownership and management. And some personalities, quite apart from compensation, can function well only in an environment of individual enterprise. But the probabilities are that most youngsters will want to chart the safer course.

Even your children who are entering one of the professions probably will succumb to the security of a salary. Both government and industry have many opportunities for the physician, dentist, lawyer and architect. For those who may prefer private practice there are partnerships and associations available to assure the newcomer a quicker and more lucrative practice.

As we have said, there will continue to be a place in our system for enterprising individuals, but that action we commonly call "individual enterprise"—the practice of "going into business for yourself"—is rapidly becoming, if not obsolete, at least much less frequently encountered. As a general practice the trades and crafts are now too complex—and too costly—for the individual operator.

Twenty-five years ago the young man with some facility at writing, a little sales ability, a little merchandising experience, could rent an office, call himself an "advertising agent," and go out after accounts. Most of our larger advertising agencies were launched in just about that fashion.

Today the one-man advertising agency is out. You need a research department, specialists in radio and television, a space-buyer, an art director, a copy chief—and maybe a consulting psychologist on a part-time basis. All this runs into money, and you'd better see at least a million dollars' worth of billing in the offing before you sign a long-term lease.

Along with everything else, the cost of launching a new business has become stratospheric. Only recently a young publisher of my acquaintance, who started a small venture shortly after World War II with a capital of $200,000, expressed doubt

that he could get going today on the same modest scale for half
a million dollars.

We may regret and deplore this state of affairs, but the im-
mutable fact remains: *you don't do it on a shoestring any more.*

It requires no special perception to see which way the wind
blows. Pick out a county-seat town at random. Walk around the
courthouse square. Note the branch stores and chain operations.
Twenty-five years ago there were none to speak of. Another
twenty-five years and you will see only a sprinkling of smart
independent merchants bucking the trend. Sure, maybe your
kid can be one of these smart ones. But if he's just a little smarter
he probably will be managing one of the chain outlets, with
more money and fewer ulcers.

These persistent individualists in business—and in many of the
professions—bring to mind the case of a rural neighbor of mine
who recently received a call from a government agent.

The government man had dropped in to see that my farmer
neighbor was complying with all the minimum-wage regulations.

"Well," said the farmer complacently, "my two hired hands
is out in the barn somewheres; the woman that does the house
chores is in the kitchen, I reckon. You can go and talk with 'em
if you're a mind to."

The agent went his way and presently returned. Everything,
he reported, seemed to be in order. One hand was getting a
dollar and a quarter an hour and his meals. The other was getting
a dollar an hour, a five-room house, a vegetable patch, and two
quarts of milk a day; the maid got thirty dollars a week, her room,
board, and some fringe benefits.

"Anybody else working around here?" asked the government
guy, as he prepared to move on to his next assignment.

"Well, only the half-wit," concluded the farmer. "He gits ten
dollars a week for tobacco and spending money."

"Ten dollars a week!" exploded the agent. "Why, that's the

worse case of exploitation I ever heard of. Let me talk to that man!"

"Well, mister," said the farmer mildly, "you're atalkin' to him right now!"

And so we come now toward the end of an era. We may come reluctantly, but we come relentlessly. A new period is beginning for our children—an era which we can as yet discern only in vague and indefinite outline. But at this distance we must try with all our perceptive powers to "see it plain." For only as we are able to get some conception of the world that is to be can we guide and counsel those young people in our charge, preparing them as best we may for the challenges of a changing course.

We—the adults of this passing hour—are the last generation to personify what Herbert Hoover so often and so fondly termed "rugged individualism." As the era departs we may bow to convention, giving it our glowing tributes and our flowing tears. But it was not, if the truth is told, a very good time for most of the human family.

The trouble with rugged individualism is that too many individuals are not rugged enough to take it. Ours has been a time of Great Pretense, with Horatio Alger as the Archbishop of Artifice. We told our young people that the Road to Realization was an open highway and all who wished might reach the golden goal.

It wasn't true. By the very nature of things only one, or two, or perhaps three in a hundred are destined for fame and fortune. These few need no prodding preachments or inspirational tomes. The mark of destiny is on them and come what may they will find their way.

A young musician once approached Mozart and sought some suggestions on the technique of composing an opera.

"You are," said Mozart, "much too young and inexperienced to fashion an opera."

"But," said the other impatiently, "you composed an opera at the age of fourteen."

"Ah, yes," agreed Mozart, "but I didn't ask how."

And so it is with those of exceptional talent in any age. They ask neither our consent nor our aid. They know where they are going, and why.

But what of the vast majority of the human family who can never hope to climb too far out of the mire of mediocrity? We haven't done very well by them in our era of "free enterprise" and "rugged individualism." They are pretty wonderful people and without them there couldn't be much of a world. But we have fed them moldy fables, marred their vision with unrealistic objectives, and too tragically often filled them with feelings of frustration and failure because they find themselves at middle age leading the routine, honest lives they were born to live.

Surely the next generation can do better than that! The one simple truth I should like to see us impart to our children now, in the early formative years, is this: You can have a great deal of fun on the merry-go-round even if you never catch a golden ring.

I have heard it charged of late that this young generation is preoccupied with security; that a prospective employee is given these days to inquiries concerning a company's pension plan and related benefits.

I hope that this is true. It is a cheering portent and I hear it gladly. It denotes a healthy, realistic turn of mind. Instead of bemoaning a lack of "ambition" the queried employer should take satisfaction in the knowledge that here is a youngster obviously intent upon a prolonged period of faithful service.

And what should concern a young person of rather commonplace talents more than the social services an employer provides now and for the future? Insurance statistics disclose that seven persons in ten, at retirement age, are dependent solely upon relatives, social security or public charity. Our young worker may be one of the fortunate three—but it isn't a very good gamble.

As we have seen, the exceptional individuals are going to take care of themselves. It's nice to give them a helping hand. Our encouragement is a strengthening factor. But they'll get where they are going whether the course is strewn with cushions or cobblestones.

It is the others—the many, many others—who present a problem. (And your children probably are included!) In the name of common sense, and with a humble respect for the innate dignity of the human species, let's tell our young people the truth. Throw away the silly platitudes, the half-baked inspirational tomes. Quit preaching to a kid that success lies in getting to the top, when he obviously doesn't have—and never can acquire— what it takes to get there. This is not only nonsense, it is cruel, barbaric stupidity.

Success *doesn't* lie in getting to the top. Success lies in living up to one's capabilities, whether those capabilities are great or small. No matter who comes in first, you win your race if you run as fast as you are able.

Fame and fortune are trinkets for the few. But happily Mother Nature has been generous in her distribution of talents. We all have our points of distinction. We can do some one thing better than it commonly is done. Encourage your children to develop and cherish these minor talents. They are the compensations God gives us for marching behind the second band in the big parade.

Your child may never set the world on fire, but neither will he "burn up" with frenzied frustrations, so long as there is the knowledge that he is the best danged tenor in Rockdale County and no one in the neighborhood can pitch a better game of horseshoes. These are the distinctions that lighten and brighten the lives of ordinary people in what is, for the most part, a very ordinary world.

In this day when children may have a somewhat broader education than their parents (and that is likely to be true even though the parents are college graduates) there is a danger that we may be overawed by this superficial brilliance; that we may make plans for a child that are beyond his inclination or capacity.

The primary purpose of education is to open minds. Through formal curricula and the establishment of sound habits of study we may hope to whet the intellect of an individual and thus direct him toward a more perceptive appreciation of his role as citizen of an expanding universe. But the final decision of a career is his alone.

We all know too well the parent who, thwarted in an early ambition, is determined to live vicariously by dominating the life of a child. This determination to make Johnny or Mary a "great" musician, dancer or artist is a deplorable form of cultural cannibalism. You have no right to immolate your child over the smoldering embers of your burned-out dreams.

If you would have your child bear the mark of greatness, mold him in the pattern of a great human being—tolerant, patient, perceptive, with a reverence for the dignity of man, a zest for life as it will be lived in a widening world.

III

YOUR CHILDREN IN
A WIDENING WORLD

YOUR CHILDREN WILL live their mature lives in a time of small families and steadily increasing population. Paradoxical as this may seem, it is a clearly marked trend for the remainder of the twentieth century.

How can we have a gradual reduction in the size of our families and at the same time contemplate an increase in our total population? It doesn't seem to make sense.

Here is the explanation: While the adjusted birth rate may be expected to decline—as it has been declining for a hundred and fifty years, with occasional periodic variations in the pattern —this factor is overcompensated by remarkable reductions in infant mortality and by the fact that our mature citizens are living somewhat longer lives.

Of course this condition cannot continue perpetually. We have gone about as far as we can go in reducing infant mortality (in fact, in 1957, for the first time in more than twenty years, we faced a slight *increase* in the death rate of children under five years of age). At the other end of the trail, too, there are obvious limits. Human mortality is one hundred per cent. Although we may forestall death, we cannot evade it.

There is a great deal of confusion and misunderstanding with respect to the subject of longevity. A popular conception that we have substantially lengthened the lives of our senior citizens is largely a myth. What we have done, primarily, is to reduce the death rate of individuals in all periods leading up to middle age. This has been accomplished by virtually eliminating such hazards as smallpox, diphtheria, typhoid fever, yellow fever, malaria, and more recently, to a somewhat lesser extent, tuberculosis, pneumonia and diabetes. There has been substantial progress in arresting cancer where early diagnosis and treatment have been practicable.

These are the infections, contagions and maladies that, as the old saying had it, "took men before their time." The effect of their diminution is that more people are now living longer. Today, if you do not succumb to accidental death (and accidents now rank fourth as a cause of death in our total population), your chances of reaching retirement age are greatly enhanced. And you will have lots of company. In 1900 only 4.1 per cent of our people were over 65 years of age. Today the figure is 8.1 per cent.

In the matter of actually increasing the life span there has been little real progress. One complication is that an overwhelming majority of us still are born into the world with what may be termed "fifty-seventy" constitutions. We are likely to die sometime between our fiftieth and seventieth birthdays. We are not constitutionally endowed for longer life. We lack the genes of longevity.

While an exceptional individual may, by exercising special care, extend life well beyond his constitutional endowment, most of us will not.

There are occasional rash predictions that man presently will live to an average age of one hundred years, or even longer. Responsible biologists do not concur in such conclusions. We shall first have to eliminate our hereditary constitutional limitations. And that is a slow, tedious process. "The best way to attain a venerable age," said Dr. Raymond Pearl, "is to select long-lived ancestors and take the precaution to be born into the world with a comfortable competence."

If the birth rate in the United States continues to decline to a point where it approaches the replenishment level (a condition that already obtains in most of the countries of Western Europe) and if we are unable to make significant contributions toward lengthening the life span, a process of "leveling off" is inevitable. Most demographers anticipate this as an eventual condition. But it can hardly occur in the United States before the first quarter of the next century.

This reference to a declining birth rate may mystify and confuse you. Most of the talk for some time has been of new and higher reproduction rates. Profound articles have appeared in the public prints forecasting prodigious population increases based on these recent rates. Forums have been held to inquire seriously whether population is threatening to get out of hand.

For the ten years from 1947 through 1956, our crude birth rate (the number of live births annually per thousand population) averaged 24.58. The death rate per thousand population for the same period averaged 9.62 annually. Or, to put it another way: the ratio of births to deaths was slightly better than two and one half to one.

If this condition should continue, it is obvious that population would increase at a rate far more rapid than at any time in our national history. The increase is chiefly attributable to the great number of marriages consummated in the early postwar years and to the births of second, third and fourth children in established households—births postponed because of the tensions and uncertainties of war.

There are many compelling reasons why the birth rate will stabilize at a more normal level and why the now firmly fixed pattern of the small family will prevail. This topic we shall discuss more fully in another chapter. For the moment we need

only point out that birth rates began a decline in November, 1957—too early for the business recession to have been much of a factor.

Those couples who married in the early postwar years have now, generally speaking, established their families. We have coming to maturity and marriage a generation born in the late-depression and early-war years. Since the "baby crop" was at a markedly low level during that period, these couples are reduced in number. We may consequently expect a decline in the crude birth rate for a few years to come. Another upward surge of births may be expected in ten or twelve years as the postwar generation begins family formation.

There is another point in relation to that meager "depression" generation that deserves our special attention. It will presently throw the population rather badly out of balance. In 1957 Secretary of Labor James P. Mitchell warned that, because of the low birth rate in the mid-1930's and early 1940's, we shall have in 1965 (despite a whopping increase in the total population) some 700,000 *fewer men* in the prime 25 to 34 age bracket than we had in 1957.

This is an extremely serious matter. It is the men of that age, experienced and indoctrinated, who are commonly expected to begin the assumption of directional duties and responsibilities. There just will not be enough of them to go around. The consequence of this shortage is that your children entering the labor market around 1965 will have unusual opportunities for advancement. This imbalance will continue through the 1970's and even into the 1980's. With a chronic shortage of senior executives in business and "older heads" in the professions, heavier responsibilities must rest upon relatively young shoulders.

It may be well at this point to take a look at the probable population picture for the remainder of the century. The figures have a special relevance to opportunities that will be afforded

your children in their years of maturity. Precise prognostications
are hazardous. Birth rates, as we have seen, are affected quickly
and decisively by prevailing social and economic conditions.

The reproduction rate of our next great family-formation
group—beginning around 1970—will determine our growth for
the subsequent fifty years. In the interval we can say with some
assurance that by 1965 we should have in the United States somewhere between 185 million and 200 million population. By 1975
the number should reach 215 million to 225 million.

Since figures are rather dull and somewhat difficult to compre-
hend, let us illustrate this forecast by saying that in less than
twenty years the new people in our world—the added population
—should more than twice outnumber the 1950 population of all
the New England states. They may well exceed the present
population of Chicago *plus* all the people now living in all the
states west of the Rocky Mountains.

While our population forges forward during this twenty-year
period, a condition will be developing which very few persons
even faintly suspect. Let us look into this phenomenon unique in
American history. It will exert a tremendous influence on the
lives of your children.

For the next twenty years, and probably for a much longer
period, our population will be growing almost twice as rapidly
as our labor force. While the birth rate has something to do with
this situation, it is only one segment of the over-all problem.

We must realize that the labor force is depleted by our insistence on higher education for our younger generation. In 1900
only the exceptional youth got through high school. Now a
minimum of four years of college is becoming a commonplace.
In 1954 we established a record in educational history with two
and a half million of our young people in colleges and universities. In 1958 the enrollment had jumped to three and a third
million. By 1975 the total is likely to be somewhere between

nine and twelve million, if we can build classrooms rapidly enough to accommodate all who seek admission. This is a commendable trend. We can take pride in our educational objectives. And we shall have pressing need for the specialized skills of this educated generation. Yet we must view realistically the effect on our labor market when Jane and John go to work, not at fifteen or sixteen, but at twenty-one or twenty-two.

Dr. George Gaylord Simpson, paleontologist at the American Museum of Natural History, once remarked half facetiously that in the long range man had no choice but to lengthen his life span since he must in some way compensate for the added years now spent in learning how to get ready to live.

At the same time there is another relentless drain. In 1935 Congress passed the Social Security Act, establishing retirement benefits for workers at the age of sixty-five. Although this program paid out $56 billion in benefits (including unemployment insurance) in its first twenty years of operation, the full effect of the act on our labor force is yet to be felt. The scope of Social Security has recently been broadened to embrace a much larger group of workers than originally contemplated. With an increasing percentage of our population reaching retirement age and turning to nonproductive pursuits, the deprivation will soon reach serious proportions.

One further point before we move on to summation: From its very inception this country has lived on borrowed labor. In the eighty years from 1850 to 1930 we brought in more than thirty-five million immigrants, chiefly prime-of-life workers from Europe's choicest stocks.

These were the men and women who made industrial America. Without their labor we could not in so short a time have cleared our forests, forced our transportation lines from coast to coast, and built our varied industries to a premier position in the commerce of the world. The labor of these immigrants made possible a steady rise in the living standards of all Americans.

Their high fertility mitigated for a time the declining birth rate of native stock. They are the ancestors of many present-day American citizens. Your children's children will reap the benefit of their diligence and devotion.

The flow of immigration came to an abrupt halt in the early 1930's, due to our restrictive legislation, inspired by depression and rising unemployment. In the decade from 1920 to 1930 we welcomed more than four million immigrants. In the next ten years less than half a million foreigners were able to find a haven here.

If we had not curbed immigration, the countries of Western Europe would soon have taken steps to keep their nationals at home. Our gain was Europe's drain. With a few notable exceptions, European countries now face a manpower shortage, since their populations hover at or slightly below the bare replenishment level.

Thus immigration—desirable immigration—will henceforth be, for America, a very limited avenue of access. This loss of immigrant labor would have been more keenly felt in the recent decade of industrial expansion had it not been for the vast strides in mechanization and automation forced upon us by the Second World War. Even so, we note the effect in a famine of domestic servants, handy men and manual laborers. The acute shortage of help drove us to power lawn mowers, automatic dishwashers, and innumerable do-it-yourself projects. Your children will find it increasingly necessary to adapt their lives to a lack-of-labor economy.

Industrially it is obvious that in the future fewer and fewer will be called upon to produce more and more. Your children must meet this challenge—or lower their standards of living. They can do so only by increased reliance upon mechanical power. Fortunately the power will be abundantly available.

Ours will be remembered as the century when machines achieved their unquestioned mastery over muscles. A hundred years ago, here in America, man and his animals still performed two thirds of the essential labor. By 1900 they were carrying slightly less than a third of the work load. In 1950 it was estimated that nearly 99 per cent of the total useful work-energy of the country was coming from machines.

And had it not been for these machines our mid-century standards of living would be wholly impracticable. To cite a single revealing instance: our registered motor vehicles now more than twice outnumber all the horses and mules in America in the banner year of 1915. The potential power of these mechanical horses is at least two hundred times as great.

To be sure, we waste this power wantonly, but the mere fact that we have it in such opulence is symbolic of our century. In 1903 the Wright brothers raised their first aircraft with the power of four horses. Today we harness 300 horses under a hood to carry a frail female to the corner drugstore for her package of energizing vitamins.

Before this century has expired we shall see our conventional resources augmented by power from the atom and from the sun —power abundant, diversified—and cheap. Power so plentiful that it will be put to uses we now can hardly imagine.

Automation, a force so new the very name was not in the dictionaries of the past decade, will move fast and far before your children are out of school. You should welcome this advance in their behalf. It is their great hope for a life of freedom and well-being in an expanding economy. Automation comes to rescue rather than to rob. It is at once the servant and the salvation of modern man. No machine can supplant the mind. The functions of direction, judgment and imagination become increasingly essential in a complex industrial order.

To put it simply, automation is eliminating a type of worker who, in our social system, is already rapidly eliminating himself. We are educating our young people out of drudgery. As we shall see more clearly in a later discussion, automation is providing vastly increased opportunities for new skills and improved techniques.

As far as we can now look toward the turn of the century, and beyond, there seems little reason for prolonged or widespread unemployment. Does this imply that at long last we approach the utopia of our social dreamers; that we may confidently anticipate a prolonged period of unvarying prosperity? Probably not.

We may now have the materials—and the formula—to construct a new and enduring era of economic plenitude. But the chances are we can't quite make a permanent go of it. That's because we must always reckon with the frailty of human nature. The business seesaw with its periodic ups and downs is the price we have historically paid for our economic freedom. Our children, too, will pay that price if they become too greedy and grasping—hypnotized by the febrile atmosphere of expansion; if they sell this year's automobiles to next year's prospects or build factories faster than markets materialize. In such situations we shall continue to have depressions, recessions, or whatever circumlocution a new generation may invent to disguise the fact that the pace has carried them too far too fast.

Even in periods of general prosperity there will be, as there always have been, minor displacements as industries become decadent and obsolete. We are beginning to educate a generation of technicians, skilled in general procedures rather than in limited crafts. Thus they can adapt themselves readily to other employment. For tomorrow's displaced worker it will be a case of changing occupation rather than vocation.

It is prudent to keep in mind that full employment does not preclude hardship. Many of us have learned to our distress that a regular paycheck is only a limited hedge against steadily rising prices. To the next generation a graver threat than unemployment is an insidious inflation that may rob them of some of the rewards of their labor. A scarcity of produce may be as devastating in its effect as a prolonged strike or lockout. The only evasion lies in more—and more effective—production.

Because modern transportation has reduced the time element in travel, making it possible for us to journey more rapidly from Here to There, we sometimes say, thoughtlessly, that the world is growing smaller. Quite the reverse is true. The world that is our concern, and must become increasingly the concern of our children, grows larger year by year.

Our fathers sang of Greenland's icy mountains and India's coral strands—and knew little or nothing of either area. Today we base our defenses on Greenland and aid India in her economic revolution.

At the turn of the twentieth century nearly two thirds of the world's inhabitants were uncivilized. Gradually we are changing that picture. We are the first generation to live in what may, with some measure of accuracy, be termed a civilized world. Some phases of our civilizing influence may be open to question. As Harold Coffin has satirically observed: "Things are coming to a pass where you can now hardly find a tribe so savage and so backward that they still slay their enemies with bows and arrows!"

Nevertheless, we have begun to alter the life pattern of a very sizable segment of the human race. Advancing this pattern must of stern necessity become a primary task of our young people for the next fifty years.

This is a matter not only of trade but of social salvation as well. The Soviet Union has openly expressed a determination to outstrip the United States industrially within a brief space of years. And, as Dr. Dennis J. Carney, an engineer returning from the Soviet steel area in 1957, pointed out: "Where the Russians sell steel, they also sell Communism." This threat must be countered with practical demonstrations of democracy in action.

With our European friends rapidly becoming self-sufficient,

and in some instances even keen competitors in our own Western Hemisphere, the one great opportunity for advancement in world trade lies in supplying the growing needs of underdeveloped peoples. This subject we pursue more fully in a subsequent chapter on "The Coming War of Wares."

Here we may say only that we must move quickly into these areas with Yankee enterprise, ingenuity and perspicacity. We must set up shop in distant lands, partnering these people in the development of their natural resources. The determined dollar must everywhere meet the ruthless ruble. And the missionaries of our ideology must be no less resourceful than those of the Soviet. This is an undertaking that involves not a mere handful of traders but an entire people, organized and unified—alert to the opportunities for the victor; fully cognizant of the consequences of defeat.

This, then, is the challenge that confronts your children—their determined destiny in a widening world.

IV THE SCHOOLED GENERATION:

Education Loses Its Luster

IN THE YEAR 1900 less than 18 per cent of our adults, aged twenty-five years or over, had received the equivalent of a high school education. Half a century later, in 1950, the figure had risen to 28.3 per cent. In another generation we doubtless shall have reversed the percentage figure of 1900 and will be able to say that less than 10 per cent of our educable adults have *not* completed high school. This "fractious fraction" who remain untutored will represent those unruly or unperceptive youngsters who simply lack the ability to absorb formal education beyond an elementary level. Within our decade educators and jurists are coming to an agreement that it is pointless to confine such youths to classrooms for a specified number of years. As yet legislation lags a bit behind informed opinion, but the time is not distant when we shall come to accept the point of view summarized by Dr. Margaret Mead: "Every child who isn't learning anything, who is miserable, and raising Cain, should be taken out of school at age fourteen and allowed to go to work."

Those who are now coming to authority in America may justly be termed our first schooled generation. Anyone among us who has attained the age of fifty will readily recall a period when our world, at least in its more mechanistic manifestations, was dominated by graduates of what Elbert Hubbard, himself an alumnus, picturesquely termed "The University of Hard Knocks." Our industrialists of the era of Henry Ford and Charlie Schwab had for the most part come up from the apprentice system. Our merchants and manufacturers were self-made men. In a typical county-seat town the school board was likely to be dominated by some aggressive characters who themselves had less formal education than many of the pupils whose destiny they in some degree shaped.

Oddly paradoxical personalities, these men were for the most part fiercely resolved to give the children of a rising generation educational advantages they themselves had been denied.

Yet they remained openly scornful of the educated youth, particularly when he sought to invade the marts of trade. Periodicals of the time were full of jokes and jibes in which the smart lad just out of college was given his comeuppance. In one typical anecdote the newly employed youth was given a broom and told to sweep out the office. "But," he protested, "this is no work for me; I have an A.B. degree." "In that case," responded the employer, taking the broom in his own hand, "come along and I'll teach you the rest of the alphabet." There was also considerable raillery concerning the cost of education and the paucity of benefits. The collegian was typically portrayed as a playboy, a wastrel, a dilettante. Though basically a serious-minded group, the student body rather relished this distorted portrait and were not above making their own contribution to further the public impression. In the case of the educational institution presided over by my father, I recall vaguely a bit of doggerel appearing in one of the student periodicals during the first decade of the century. The precise wording has slipped my mind but it concerned an agriculturist whose son made the university football team rather than the Honor Roll:

> *Consider the case of Farmer Brown,*
> *His story's sad, alack!*
> *He spent a thousand dollars*
> *And got a quarterback.*

On the whole our attitude toward education was one of respect not infrequently mingled with irreverence. Our citizens with little education continued to dominate in mundane matters for the very practical reason that there were not enough educated persons to take over. Those with high school diplomas, and the relatively few who possessed college training, had to be preserved for our professions and to man our educational bastions.

From the turn of the century through the First World War, educated persons still comprised a marked minority. In every community the preacher and the teacher were counted individuals of worth and wisdom. One gladly journeyed twenty miles and listened agape to some learned lecturer. This was the pedestrian age of communication; a time when our men in public life were presumed to know more about the world and its ways than did those of us who occupied the folding chairs grouped around the bandstand at the Fourth of July celebration.

And then almost imperceptibly the scene changed. Suddenly we came to a realization that in these times "everybody is educated." This, we should warn, is a deceptive generality. And the time now is at hand to clarify our terms.

As we have seen, in 1950 less than a third of our adults had completed high school. To be sure, the old-timers who held our average down are now disappearing from the scene. A steadily increasing percentage of our young people are getting at least twelve years of formal education. But we must keep in mind that even the compulsory education laws in a majority of states present no guarantee that bright young people, earnestly desiring an education, will be permitted to complete high school. To be sure, most of them nowadays—even when confronted by adverse circumstances—manage to make the grade. But this has been true only since the benefits of Social Security became widely available. Prior to 1935, when the Social Security Act became law, the loss of the breadwinner in a household meant, more often than not, that a high school student would have to give up his studies to join the ranks of the wage earners.

Beyond the high-school range we still ponder the question of who shall go on to college and how they shall get there. Most of you who read these pages have always taken college as an obvious step for your brood. The children of your friends and neighbors, too, are partaking of or destined for higher education. This leads naturally to the supposition that college has become a universal boon. Certainly such is not the case. According to the most recent estimates available, about a fourth of our high school graduates with the highest IQs will get no college training whatever. Of course the situation is improving. When dependable statistics are available, the decade between 1950 and 1960 will disclose that the number of college graduates has practically doubled in relation to our total population. So long as our functional illiterates (persons with less than five years of schooling) continue to outnumber all Americans holding college degrees, as they presently do, we can take no great pride in educational statistics.[1] The most dependable estimates available indicate that by 1975, roughly fifteen years hence, college graduates still will comprise less than 10 per cent of our adult population; the illiterate group will have shrunk to about 4 per cent.

One of the most realistic ways of determining where we stand educationally is to take a look at school enrollments. In the 1958–59 school year we enrolled some 42 million persons for formal instruction. About 30 million of these were students in the elementary grades; 9 million were in high schools, and slightly

[1] The 1957 statistics were: illiterates, 9.1 per cent of the adult population; college graduates, 7.7 per cent.

more than 3 million were in colleges and universities, including the graduate, technical and vocational schools.

To carry the analysis a step further, we find that in the fall of 1958 more than 4 million youngsters started school for the first time, while for the same period our total enrollment of freshmen in institutions of higher education was well under a million. Certainly some allowance must be made for the booming baby crop of recent years, which has the effect of increasing enrollment in the elementary grades. On the other hand, we must realize that many college freshmen will waver and wilt by the wayside. Thus it seems fairly safe to assume that of the 4 million who now start school annually not more than a million will eventually graduate from a college or university.

It will come as something of a shock to fond parents to realize that of four tiny tots advancing from kindergarten to the serious business of acquiring an education only one is destined to attain a degree in an institution of higher learning. It is pertinent— rather than impertinent—to inquire as to where and how the others are sidetracked.

There is a rather firmly fixed impression in cultivated minds that people in this enlightened age want all the education they can get; that any lapses or lacks in the individual's academic program are a consequence of insuperable obstacles. According to this concept, every young man and young woman in the land would turn gladly to the halls of learning if only funds could be made available for their continued education. This is a pleasant philosophy but it just doesn't jibe with the facts at the outset of this sixth decade of the twentieth century. The depressing truth is that a greater number of our young people than it is comfortable to contemplate are indifferent or actively antagonistic to education. They neither want nor are able advantageously to absorb more than a high school education. It is with a feeling of infinite relief that they lay aside hated textbooks at seventeen or eighteen and turn to the serious business of making a living.

Another group of rather substantial size would take a little more education if it came along as a gratuity. They would *like* to go on to college, but their motivation is weak. They won't make the sacrifices or take risks for the sake of a long-range gain. This attitude on the part of young high school graduates— including some very bright ones—leads to the circumstance that all over the land our educational institutions are piling up loan funds with few takers.

The National Defense Education Act, passed by the Eighty-fifth Congress in the fall of 1958, further implements the funds available for student loans. Under the provisions of this law a student may borrow $1,000 a year, or up to a total of $5,000, for college expenses. The loan is to be repaid over a period of ten years, starting one year after leaving college. Time spent in military service (up to three years) is not counted in this proposal. The interest charge is a modest 3 per cent. If the student elects to take up a career of teaching (grade or high school), 10 per cent of the loan will be "forgiven" for each of the first four years of teaching service.

These are not in any direct sense "government loans" although the United States government will add $9 for each dollar presently in the college loan fund. The school controls and administers all loans.

These liberal provisions now make it possible to say, for perhaps the first time in our history, that no young person earnestly desiring a college education—and with a mental capacity to utilize the instruction—need be denied.

And yet, distressing as it may be to make the admission, we must point out that this generous gesture by a benevolent government probably will have no very marked effect on college and university enrollments beyond the normal and rather healthy rate of increase we have been showing in recent times.

I have often had occasion to discuss with high school seniors the availability and advantages of loans for a college education. Their responses are so standardized that one might almost imagine them to be recorded and memorized. The boy will say candidly that he has no wish to "waste" another four years. He wants to get a job with some good outfit and start working his way up. Getting in on the ground floor at an early age, the company pension plan will permit him to retire before he is old and broken. Then in due course Social Security will add its mite to assure a serene old age.

You point out to these lads that today, according to accepted statistics, a college education is worth from $100,000 to $150,000 to the student in increased lifetime earnings. "Quit school now," the counselor warns, "and by the time you're thirty, the boys in your age bracket who go on and graduate from college will be forty per cent ahead of you in monthly earnings."

"Well, maybe so," agrees the student, "but taxes will take a big slice out of that added income. Besides, I want to get married and start raising a family. I don't want to saddle my wife and children with a big debt for my education that it will take the best years of our lives to pay off."

The girls present a somewhat similar recital, concluding with the virtuous declaration, "I won't carry a debt to my husband."

What has happened, slowly and almost imperceptibly, in our times is that, in practical effect, "everybody has moved backward a notch." Today the young man or woman with a high school diploma is approximately in the position of a grade school graduate a generation ago. For the foreseeable future the high school graduate will be called upon to forward the bulk of the nation's work. And so increasingly complex have these tasks become that he, like the Red Queen in *Through the Looking-Glass,* will have to run as fast as ever he can merely to keep the same place.

If, as we have just pointed out, the high school graduate is now approximately in the position of yesterday's grade school alumnus, the young man or woman now needs a college degree in order to be eligible for opportunities equivalent to those a high school diploma once offered.

Some years ago we spoke of attaining a college education. Now the talk is all of degrees. The degree—bachelor's, master's, doctor's—has become, as Theodore Clevenger once pointed out, a sort of glorified union card; with it you qualify for the job, without it you haven't a chance.

A significant consideration is the rate at which we are producing these degrees. In a nation that has just about doubled its population in fifty years, we have increased the number of our bachelor-master degrees approximately eleven times; the number of our doctorate degrees has increased twenty-two fold.

This does not signify overproduction. The need for these learned youth still outpaces the supply but mass production has inevitably taken some distinction from the diploma. What with the generally lowered academic standards—an inescapable concomitant of quantity output—the college diploma has become little more than a certificate of moderate persistence and acceptable deportment. Yet it remains the treasured symbol of the job seeker. "Nowadays," says Henry J. Taylor, the economic commentator, "if you don't have a sheepskin you might as well be naked."

"A college education isn't essential," declares one of my cynical friends, "just being a graduate sometimes will do."

Yet it would be a mistake to assume from these caustic observations that our institutions of higher education are indifferent to their obligations or that their product taken as a whole is markedly inferior. They are doing the very best they can against obvious obstacles. And this "best" is in many instances so surprisingly good that a considerable number of us, out of school for a generation, must admit candidly that these kids could give us a tough time if we should chance to find ourselves in the competitive market today. The pertinent question, however, is not whether education is better than yesterday but whether it is good enough for tomorrow.

As more and more students pour into our colleges and universities from the high schools—and as the demand for formally educated youth shows no sign of abatement—the academic average is certain to totter and tumble. Too many, in these times, are getting into college simply because someone somewhere along the line stands ready to foot the bills. They lack the ability and the stability to absorb what professors are trying to impart. Our educators are fully aware of this condition. And so, for that matter, are future employers.

"Sure, academic standards are getting lower all the time," agreed a recruiting officer for one of the big electric companies, with whom I discussed this situation recently. "But what's to be done? We need men with at least some semblance of training. We have to have them. If we can't get Einsteins, we'll have to do with the Doaks."

With general availability and widespread application, education certainly has lost some of its early luster. Still it has gained unmistakably in utilitarian value. Where once it was reckoned an ascetic asset, now it has become the tool of the workaday world.

As we have seen, each of us now must possess a little more in the way of formal education merely to hold his relative place in line. This being the case, can we anticipate a future in which the college degree will be as prevalent as is the high school diploma in our day?

Perhaps. But this day will hardly dawn within the active lifetime of your school-age children. The practical difficulties are too obstructive. We must reckon first with the inadequate motivation of a generation not too far removed from the simple fundamentals of the three R's. Moreover, there is the realistic problem of financing. Educators are currently driven to distraction by the prospect that normal college enrollment probably will double within a decade. Even assuming that our taxpayers and philanthropists would put up the desired dollars (certainly a dubious surmise) we couldn't throw together enough walls and dig up enough instructors to send a simple majority of our high school seniors through college. They just aren't going. And that's that.

Instead of vastly increasing the number of our conventional college graduates beyond, of course, such advances as normally increasing population dictates, a more probable development of the next generation would appear to be the practice of sending more persons to college for shorter periods of time.

This will be an outgrowth of the developing trend in numerous occupations and vocations to demand some cultural schooling as a prelude to technical instruction. It is an extension of the practice which we began in the nineteenth century of requiring formal education for the votaries of our more exacting professions. There are persons alive today who can recall clearly when a physician, a surgeon, a lawyer or an architect could enter his calling through the apprentice system with an extremely sketchy educational background. And these early practitioners, more often than not, had incredibly elementary facilities. (My mother, as a young student at Tennessee Wesleyan University in the late 1880's, had a tooth filled by a traveling dentist who cleaned the cavity with the small blade of a pocketknife and mixed the amalgam on a longer blade. The filling, incidentally, served her for more than forty years.)

You may have heard, with perhaps some suggestion of derision, the statement that "one even needs a college degree these days in order to become an undertaker." This is only a partial exaggeration. An increasing number of states now require two years of liberal arts study in a recognized college as a prelude to technical training in the art of embalming.

That this requirement is no mere affectation—no useless appendage—is pointed out by Dr. Charles O. Dhonau, dean of the Cincinnati School of Embalming. "We have found," he tells me, "that the unschooled, or the inadequately educated, do not communicate well with their peers when they get out into the wider world. In a profession such as ours, where human relations are paramount, the leavening force of a liberal arts education is no luxury. It is becoming a practical necessity. That is why we co-operate actively with legislators in every effort to raise educational standards in the several states."

Very much the same sentiment has been expressed by Dean Karl L. Kaufman of the Butler University School of Pharmacy when he went so far as to tag pharmacists lacking in liberal arts background as "technical barbarians."

This trend toward cultural emphasis in vocationalism has little more than begun; it will be increased to cover a great many additional callings in the years immediately ahead, while your younger children still are school-bound.

One salutary effect of this movement is that it will tend to revive interest in and revitalize the liberal arts courses in our schools, particularly in the freshman and sophomore years. For a period of fifteen or twenty years—and notably since the "Sputnik scare"—technical courses have tended to obscure and at times, it has almost seemed, threatened to obliterate the humanities.

A study I made in 1954 of the requirements laid down by corporation recruiting officials visiting one Middle-western university indicated that scarcely one in nine had any interest in the liberal arts graduate. Last year a similar survey showed approximately three in ten calling for prospects with "some majors in the liberal arts."

While this still shows a rather large preponderance of recruiters interested in the technicians, it is not an accurate gauge of the interest in or place for the liberal arts graduate. A waiting world still is assimilating all such persons as rapidly as they become available. It is just that competition for their services is not so keen as in some other areas. After all, a big corporation isn't going to spend from $75 to $100 a day to send a man to the campus to interview prospective employees as long as it is reasonably certain of acquiring its quota without this investment.

In my judgment the tide has begun to turn—and will turn increasingly—back toward pursuit of the liberal arts—the humanities. Do not discourage or dissuade your child who shows a natural tendency toward, let us say, philosophy or sociology. After all, we shall need all types of talent to operate successfully a world that grows increasingly complex and varied. Do not mar a promising poet in a febrile but unavailing effort to produce a Pasteur. Parents, it has seemed to me, should not contribute to the current clatter to turn our classrooms into recruiting stations for the wholesale production of robots equipped with slide rules. Certainly we must hearten our youth of promising potential to turn their talents and their time toward scientific endeavors. But let us be mindful of the fact that in a balanced social order there will be need for logic as well as logarithms; for merchants as well as mathematicians. And the typewriter may prove a tool quite as essential in its way as the test tube.

As mentors for a rising generation our prime responsibility perhaps is to remain forever cognizant of the vast powers of natural selection. Let us curb the messianic impulse, the compulsive urge, remembering that the good shepherd follows the sheep, his province to guard them from pitfalls rather than to chart a precise course.

"The aim of American education," said an Ohio schoolman to whom I listened with rising ire, "should be to make eggheads out of everybody."

This is one of those epigrammatic observations that tend to lose cogency upon analysis. For one thing, the compulsive connotation is suspect. It is reminiscent of that turn-of-the-century era when a father judicially ruled, "We will make a preacher out of Tom, a doctor of Dick and a lawyer of Harry."

Education is overburdened with directives. But assuredly its mission and its justification lie in tutoring the human spirit to live tranquilly and effectively in a world that is ever chaotic and often confused.

The aim of the American educational system should not be to *make* anything out of anybody. The first purpose of education is to open minds. "The mark of an educated man is to see something in a mud puddle besides mud." Through formal curricula and the establishment of sound habits of study, we may hope to whet the intellect of an individual, be he potential pundit or plumber. Thus we may direct him toward a more perceptive appreciation of his role as citizen of an expanding universe.

V   THE GREAT MYTH OF THE ONE-CLASS SOCIAL SYSTEM

ONE OF THE canons of the ancient Christian Church once drew a rather materialistic view of heaven. There at a sumptuous banquet board sat all the major saints, forever eating. Ranged back of these exalted ones were multiplied rows of lesser saints, all engaged in digesting, digesting, digesting.

Nowadays, as I enter a modern supermarket and observe the countless array of articles attractively packaged for my enticement, I am tempted to think of this old writer and his vision of heaven. Except, of course, that here the work of "digesting" or preparing the foods has been done for us in advance. Carrots have lost their feathery tops; potatoes have been scrubbed to a pristine cleanliness; some foods are precooked in the natural state, others fast-frozen, so that on short notice a housewife may readily concoct the best meal you ever thaw. Moreover, the content of books and magazines has been condensed to give us their essence in an eyeful.

Since we have achieved this state of standardization, someone has suggested that the next step inevitably will be "packaged people." That is, we shall have men and women who share the same motivation; who have substantially the same tastes and desires; eat the same foods; wear identical apparel; participate in the same recreations; react in somewhat the same way to the same stimuli when manipulated by a potent persuader. In short, we all are growing very much alike. And with a beneficent government stimulating incomes at one end and arbitrarily limiting them at the other, we even are coming, so the observers assure us, to a state of "classless" society where, in the words of the Kingfish, "we all will be brothers in one great fraternity."

Well, let us take a look at this conformity pattern, see what it is and where it promises to lead us.

History, unhappily, has not preserved the identity of the individual who, overwhelmed by the grandeur of a scenic view, resolved to bring it indoors. His concept of the picture window was brilliant, imaginative—and widely copied. Friends and neighbors came to see, and went away to construct windows of their own. Some lacked the view, but that was a minor matter. They had the window anyway. Thus we have come to an absurd finality where we fashion picture windows in our living rooms merely to peer into the picture windows of our opposite numbers across the street.

There we have in capsule content the history of American conformity. And yet conformity is not in the inherent nature of man. He infinitely prefers to be an innovator, a launcher, a leader. A difficulty arises in the fact that he lacks the imaginative quality to originate. For every innovator there are a hundred improvisers, a thousand who can only copy.

So, for the most part, we go along, swiping as judiciously as we can, as brazenly as we dare. Not because we have any real desire to conform or follow a beaten path; but, on the contrary, with the hope that by appropriating selected ideas from remote sources we may perhaps reflect a little of the credit that is bestowed upon the innovator. It may not be an especially worthy ambition but it is a universal one.

In some areas of life we all are perpetrators of the pattern.

It is not, generally speaking, our effort to "keep up with the Joneses," as the colloquial phrase has it, that makes difficulties for us. More frequently it is the determination to keep one up on Mr. Jones and his household that leads to an endless succession of difficulties.

The point is well presented in a story of two advertising agency vice-presidents, neighbors in a swank New York suburb, who carried on an intense rivalry to attain and sustain a measure of personal prestige. Any possession one acquired the other would seek to surpass.

When Art bought a new Jaguar, Dan was soon driving an even flashier model of the same make.

As the next move, Dan received a phone call. "Hi!" exclaimed a familiar voice. "This is your neighbor, Art. I'm calling from my car."

So Dan not only had to have a phone in *his* car; he was impelled to call Art in his Jaguar to point out that this new phone was a precise match for the car's upholstery.

Art was nonplused. But for only a moment. "Well, now, Danny Boy," he enthused, "that's real enterprising of you. Er— hold on a moment, will you? I'll have to answer my *other* phone." Probably not many of us plank down our long green on the counter for the primary, conscious purpose of arousing a comparable cast in the countenance of a neighbor. Yet this pleasure of inducing envy is one of the undeniable though transient satisfactions of a prestige purchase. Transient, yes, because it is only a matter of time before the neighbors will match or surpass our acquisition. The total action, therefore, serves merely to emphasize rather than mitigate our conformity.

So, in brief review, we have seen that man, by nature, is not a conformer. Yet much of the time he is forced into that role, primarily because he has nothing better to offer. Egged by his females to refurbish the nest, he will come up with a set of living-room furniture very like that recently purchased by the

Jones family—not that he wants to ape the Joneses—he'd infinitely prefer to outdo them—but with his rather limited imagination this turned out to be the best thing he could buy at the price he could afford to pay. Everything now is serene, let us hope. And everyone has settled down to a state of tranquil bliss.

But no. For what is that disturbance in the back yard? It is the hubbub of excavators preparing for the construction of a new swimming pool for the Jones family. That Jones boy just won't be nailed down.

Not that Jones is an individual. He is a type. And in certain situations under certain conditions he takes on something of your own mien. For we all like to show off our possessions, to show up our neighbors, and as readily as we can, to advance ourselves rung by rung up the social ladder.

How much validity is there in the contention that we are advancing toward a one-class social order? Well, beyond question there are great forces at work leavening and leveling our financial peaks and valleys. The rich are getting a little poorer, the poor are a good deal richer.

However, to conclude from the foregoing that there has been or will be a vast upheaval in our social order is a hasty and somewhat unwarranted conclusion. Of course, the whole social structure is constantly undergoing a process of change. People are moving from one stratum to another. And for the most part they move upward. This is not merely, or even primarily, a matter of money. Not that we are belittling money, you understand. It is one of the desirables, even one of the essentials, for you and your children. But in an era where everyone has money other desiderata take on added significance. A crude, ungracious person who is well-heeled becomes merely a boor with a bank balance. Sooner or later he will be placed by the inexorable judgment of his peers into an appropriate social niche.

What we are trying to say in simple terms is that the fact that more people have more money does not automatically elevate the multitude in our social order; it merely cheapens money as a social factor. In a pioneer order where, broadly speaking, no one had money, social distinctions prevailed. They will prevail even in an order where "everyone" has money.

My friends who see in this matter of gradually doing away with grinding poverty the development of a vast one-class social system are, I believe, basically mistaken. For there are discrepancies in the human species that defy all efforts at standardization. A sociologist of my acquaintance had an unusual opportunity to observe this truth in practice during the course of World War II. A thousand families—strangers to each other—were moved into a government-created community. With a handful of exceptions they were similarly housed and received approximately the same compensation. Yet it was fascinating to observe how quickly social circles developed. People with similar social backgrounds naturally gravitated to each other. Soon there were social lines as hard and fast as those drawn in any county-seat community. And money, practically speaking, did not enter into the consideration.

James, my handy man, drives a better car than I feel I can afford. Perhaps it is a better car than he can afford. That is a matter between James and the man at the finance company. The possession of this car is important to my handy man. And I have no doubt that it procures for him a better type of girl friend. But the fact that he drives a splendid car makes it less imperative for me to do so. Nowadays a Cadillac at the curb signifies little beyond the fact that the owner has, transiently at least, made peace with the installment house. It is no longer a symbol denoting superior social status. The split-level residences of the butcher's son and the baker's daughter now back cozily up to the suburban home of the electric-light maker (who has had to sell off most of his acreage for a subdivision because he can no longer afford to maintain an estate).

This circumstance neither deprives nor assures the butcher-baker progeny social equality with their neighbor. Whether they "fit in" with the new environment will depend on many factors. Money is by no means the only catalyst in this social transition.

"Money cannot buy happiness, contentment and social preferment," says one of my ironic friends. "Of course," he then concludes, "my reference is to Confederate money."

Sometimes to the superficial observer it does appear that money is carrying a great many people a very great way.

"I resent these upstarts who are moving into my world," declares a young acquaintance, the product of several generations of gracious living. "Suddenly they are making everything crowded and uncomfortable. I simply can't reconcile myself to the conviction that they belong."

To this observation we can only say, for such solace as it may afford, that a good many of these "intruders" obviously don't belong and never will. For we now are going through a transition period that will continue at least through the lifetime of your children. In this situation the term "upstart" is a singularly appropriate one. It signifies that these newcomers are just starting up. How far they can travel depends much more upon personal traits and innate character than upon financial resources. Money is only one of the elements from which we build a successful, well-rounded life. And no one knows this quite so well as that bitterly disillusioned group who have nothing else.

There are, however, comforts in conformity that must not be minimized. Eventually we may adopt or adapt the ideas or ideals of our innovators, but these deviates themselves rarely are beloved citizens. This is especially true where their example involves profound changes in our habits and habitats. The Carol Kennicotts may in the long run alter the course of our lives. But they don't win any popularity contests.

If anybody is going to bring newfangled notions into our settlement, we ourselves want to do the toting. The stranger with a yen to point a Better Way of Life will get short shrift. And this resistance to change would appear to be in direct ratio to the congestion of our populations; the close communal pattern of our lives. It is for this reason, primarily, that I sense a slowly growing lack of development in expressions of individuality in the steady advance of our closely knit suburban lives.

In such situations conformity is more than a convenience. It becomes almost a compulsion. The slight deviation unnoted in a remote neighbor is a glaring eccentricity when distances are reduced and common interests multipled. Where half a dozen families live within a stone's throw, someone is likely to go in for slingshot practice.

A number of years ago, when I was conducting a survey in a tenement district, several tenants spoke in obvious disdain of a neighbor. Subsequently I met the object of their derision and found her to be a gentle lady who, through a piece of misfortune, had been reduced to lodgings in a blighted area. Obviously out of her element, she was disliked and distrusted because her way of life was alien to their own.

It is of course an exaggeration to refer to certain of our real estate developments in the near-suburbs as the Tenements of our Times. There is, nevertheless, a tenuous connection. Many of these families, clustered in their tiny prefabs with the propinquity of biscuits in an oven, have recollections—and roots—on the wrong side of the tracks.

A sociologist studying conditions in one of the larger subdivisions on the edge of Chicago relates a revealing incident. A housewife in one of the more thickly populated courts told of a young couple who a few months previously had moved into their block. Obviously eager to make friends and get along in a new environment, the wife invited a few of the neighbor women in for an afternoon party. "She did everything wrong," the suburban veteran explained. "The girls showed up in their slacks and swimming suits—the customary afternoon attire—and here this newcomer trotted out her doilies and her best china."

After this experience, it seems, the neighbors systematically excluded the couple—and even their child—from all social functions. The discouraged family finally moved back to Chicago. A rather harsh penalty, it would seem, for the crime of endeavoring to introduce some of the simpler amenities into the barren social pattern of a community. In our modern communal life the pressures can be relentless. If the deviate's social behavior is markedly below the group average—and (especially in the near-in congested suburbs) that average can be pretty low—some compassion may be shown. There are those ready and willing to give the underprivileged a helping hand. But if some tactless act of a newcomer tends to spotlight the barrenness and sterility of the aggregate life pattern, beware! The group will at once consolidate and drum the offender out of their community.

To assume that gestures leading toward compulsive conformity are restricted to the congested, low-priced subdivisions would be a serious error. Retribution of the offender is there merely exercised more promptly and in a somewhat more primitive form. Most of our suburbs are now developing their mores, and their motivations, to see that the regulations are exercised and the deviates exorcised. That all this may be done in a semi-jocular manner is merely a manifestation of upper-class urbanity. The one who has strayed a little out of line has no difficulty in getting the point.

A senior executive in a middle-western city moved to one of the moderately exclusive suburbs. A couple of weeks after he had settled down in the new environment and was beginning to do some puttering around in the yard, a neighbor sauntered over for a sociable chat.

"Joe," said the established resident, after an exchange of amenities, "we all wear shorts around here when we are doing our yard work. It's a sort of community custom. If you don't get yourself some shorts, we're going to have to boycott you."

Instead of taking this as an intolerable affront to personal liberty and poking the meddling neighbor in the nose, as his father doubtless would have been disposed to do, Joe meekly went out and bought four pairs of shorts.

Then, to be sure, there is the quite unconscious conformity, the natural imitative actions of the individual within a compact group. This has always been true of the human family. A hundred years ago, when neighbors were a quarter of a mile apart, people still tended to follow similar routine patterns in their daily lives. About the only difference nowadays is that newfangled notions are more quickly assimilated, to become the accepted behavior pattern of the group.

At twilight on a summer Sabbath a friend of mine was motoring through a restricted suburban area in a Middle-western community. As he drove along he became increasingly conscious of a pungent odor pervading the atmosphere. A sudden realization dawned. His olfactory nerves were bringing evidence of a score of smoldering charcoal fires. In their sundry patios householders were heating the grills for Sunday evening steaks or hamburgers.

It is only in these late years that we have been especially concerned over our patterned existence. Through earlier periods people accepted conformity pretty much as a matter of course. Now commentators on the contemporary scene have begun to make us a trifle self-conscious of our follow-the-leader tendencies. Presently someone will be writing a textbook on the Art of Expressing Your Individuality. Soon all these restive souls will be following the standardized formula. And we shall be right back where we started.

VI THE NEW QUEST FOR COMMUNAL COGNIZANCE

AT FIRST GLANCE that title seems somewhat pretentious; a bit on the prolix side. Yet it is a rather apt description of a condition indulged in by a considerable number of Americans in our day. Disillusioned and dismayed, they are looking around for answers to the question, Why aren't people paying attention to us? These individuals have faithfully fulfilled certain commitments. They have accomplished those things that were considered essential of performance. They have reached their goals. Why, then, are they denied communal cognizance? Where are the bended knees, the respectful curtsies? Why can't the community see and readily recognize sterling characters of worth and substance?

Back about the turn of the century there used to be certain symbols that said these things for a man. Symbols that spoke eloquently and effectively. If, in a county-seat town a householder lived in a big mansion surrounded by an ample lawn and a well-kept picket fence, it was obvious to one and all that the family had money and position. They were people of importance. If, as an out-at-elbows child, you met the master of that house on the streets you probably gave him a bashful bow, or at least a deferential "sir," tacked on to your "howdy." Clearly he was someone to be looked up to.

If there was a car parked in front of that house—almost any kind of automobile—it was to be viewed as yet another symbol. This told you that the man not only had money; he was a "modern," intent upon living in his day, attuned to the tempo of his times.

Later, to be sure, the *kind* of car became increasingly revealing. In time it had to be a Locomobile, a Pierce-Arrow, and still later a Packard or a Cadillac. These were the automobiles driven by citizens who had attained dignity and distinction in the community.

Other symbols were developed through the years: signs and portents that enabled people generally to recognize and revere their more opulent or perhaps their more intellectually glittering neighbors. For respect was due the brain as well as the bank balance.

Naturally the professional people came in for an almost automatic accolade; the preachers and professors got their bows and scrapes; the few college graduates to be found outside the classroom or pulpit came in for a special reverence. In addition to these, almost anyone who had "been away to school," even if for only a term at a nearby business college, merited special consideration. A framed high school diploma in the year 1910 probably won as much adulation as would a Ph.D. degree in a modern household. And I am half persuaded that in relative terms it got its possessor just about as far along the Road to Realization.

And now the old symbols are losing their substance and significance. That faded high school diploma went rather shamefacedly to the attic twenty years ago. The big house has succumbed to a subdivision. The costly car? The one you see parked over yonder probably belongs to a house painter who makes more money than a college professor or to the operator of a newspaper route who needs a heavy car and chanced to make a fortunate buy on a used-car lot.

To be sure, the ingenious try to devise new symbols—fresh ways of saying "I am both well to do and perceptive." These are dangled before the gullible to be gobbled up at a price. But so soon do these become the claptrap of the market place that they are hardly worth the effort to acquire.

Consider the swimming pool. You need a memory scarcely longer than a stray basting thread to recall when a pool was something you encountered only in a park, surrounded, probably, by municipal guards. Oh, to be sure, a few movie stars had them out in Hollywood but people in less glamorous pursuits never thought of such a thing. And then all of a sudden they did. The back-yard swimming pool became a reality, not only in California but throughout the nation. In 1958, the industry estimates, 178,000 installations were made. A spokesman assures me that a few years hence the back-yard pool will be as common in upper middle-class households as the flower bed and may even supplant the posies if there is an acute lack of space.

Not too many years ago the greatest gaucherie a host could commit would be to throw a dinner party and then come up with a shortage of funds to meet the check. Now the host with an empty billfold is in no wise disconcerted. Flashing a card that shows he has money in the bank, or at least credit in the clearing-house, he goes blithely on his way.

Although the credit card is a fairly venerable institution in hostelries and the like, for the convenience of traveling men, its wholesale use in restaurants and marts of trade is a recent innovation. Someone conceived the notion that some discerning men might welcome the privilege of eating in certain public places "on tick" as in a private club. A few hundred fine restaurants were signed up; a few thousand membership cards were printed, and the credit clearinghouse, collecting a modest fee for its

services, was launched. How the idea has flourished is perhaps
best illustrated by a cartoon appearing in a recent issue of *The
New Yorker*. A foreign spy is apparently about to depart for an
assignment in America. His mentor gives final instructions.
"You'll find everything here, comrade—your American passport,
Social Security number, birth certificate, driver's license and
Diners' Club card." Five years ago the joke would have been
pointless. Ah, well, that illustrates the swiftness with which
symbols come and go.

Let us now return to that considerable number of Americans
who in middle life find themselves disturbed and dismayed. What
is the occasion of their distress?

It all began a long time ago. A generation coming to maturity
in the late depression years had abundant opportunity to meet
adversity on extremely intimate terms. One fact of life was clearly
impressed on these young minds: in a capitalistic social system
it is an excellent idea for the individual citizen to acquire a little
capital. So they resolved to make money. They set up certain
objectives. They observed opportunities to acquire a little more
formal education or technical training, either through conventional schools or in extension courses. They tried systematically
to get into industries where money was to be made. They exposed
themselves strategically where the lightnings of promotion would
be most likely to strike them. And it worked! Almost like a charm,
it worked. The years of the Second World War and the Korean
Incident were prosperous ones for American industry. Employment was plentiful. Wages were high. Individual entrepreneurs
flourished. Shrewd investors ticked off fat profits. To put it
succinctly, a lot of people made a lot of money. Some of the
more enterprising contrived ways and means of holding onto a
portion of their gains.

So our generation emerging from a childhood of depression
struggle found themselves at long last in comfortable circum-

stances. They had every reason to believe they now were entering a new era; about to move up a rung on the social ladder.

Cautiously they began setting up some of the trusted symbols of an earlier era. They bought an ultramodern home in one of the better suburbs. They acquired an expensive car and followed this purchase with a little foreign runabout for marketing and errands. They sent their children to the better schools. However, none of these things seemed to make a great deal of difference. The new families they met—their neighbors in the mortgaged manors—were very much like the people they had always known: small merchants and manufacturers, minor industrial executives, successful salesmen of insurance or real estate. The old symbols no longer worked. They no longer worked because, all of a sudden, there were just too many evidences of opulence. No one has time to stop and gape in awe at your particular display of affluence because they are much too absorbed in their own acquisitions.

To be sure, the crux of the matter is that our middle-class families coming out of the depression went about their money-grabbing on an individual basis, quite oblivious of the fact that the entire community—a few fixed-income unfortunates excepted —was prospering simultaneously. So, although the average individual householder and his family have admittedly profited from the comforts and niceties of modern living, he hasn't made much of a net gain in social standing. Here and there an individual of unusual personality, ability and charm has broken through the barriers. Of course that has been true in every era. The lines of social division are drawn approximately where they always have been.

Now, we have this quite large group of Americans with a sizable sum of surplus money. They are restless and resentful, vaguely embittered because, in some way they don't understand, they have been cheated out of what they consider a rightful heritage—their measure of communal cognizance.

Since there are now no longer automatic symbols of recognition for their present estate, these newcomers are thrown upon artifice and strategy. They must go to the places smart people are believed to frequent; they must do the things social leaders are reputed to do and perhaps, who knows, some accident of happy juxtaposition may lead to a fortunate connection. At the very least the folks at home may be impressed.

A matron of my acquaintance went last year to the French Riviera, believing it to be at that moment the very vortex of the social whirl. She registered at one of the more popular and expensive resorts, unpacked her bags, and began to look around. Sure enough, almost immediately, she struck up a chumship with another gay and rather dashing matron. Soon they were going places and doing things together. The second lady turned out to be a telephone supervisor from Chicago. She had thought my friend was at least a second-string Vanderbilt or a maverick of the Whitney tribe.

I have made no accurate tally, but I should not be surprised to learn that there are enough de luxe hotels, apartments and motels along Miami Beach, say in the ten-mile stretch from MacArthur Causeway northward through Hollywood, to bed down simultaneously all the genuinely prominent socialites in our ten largest cities and still have space to accommodate the individuals catalogued in the current edition of *Who's Who in America.*

That no sizable fraction of these distinguished persons is ever present in that area at any one time is obvious. Yet, night upon night, in a good season, these vast hostelries are crowded to capacity. From whence do the guests come? There can be but one answer: These sprawling habitations in a fairyland of flux and flotsam are peopled by the Pretenders. These are the eminently solvent men and women from all over America. Denied their rightful recognition at home, they flock to the resort areas in the hope of impressing other people who, in their turn, are altogether too preoccupied in an effort to impress still other groups. Some of these are wonderfully nice people, possessed of charm and endearing social attributes they have little chance to display advantageously in such a febrile, hectic and unnatural environment. Others, of course, are not so wonderful, and not so nice. One must always anticipate the crass, the vulgar, the woman with the mores of a fishwife, dragging a spouse with the morals of a fishworm.

All these Pretenders—the likable lumped with the loathsome —have a common deity to whom they make obeisance. He is that prince of the realm of Internal Revenue who makes final pronouncements relating to the beneficence of Capital Gains. Thanks to his generous provisions, the Pretenders don't have to make believe on one important score. Their money is the real thing. It had better be if they intend to unpack their bags at Fontainebleau, Eden Roc or the Diplomat.

Perhaps the greatest frustration suffered by the disappointed generation has been in their children. For a very long time there has been prevalent in this land a notion that schools make scholars; that if you send a child to an institution of learning long enough, assuming a reasonably co-operative attitude of diligence and application, he will emerge educated.

This is a premise quite short of the mark. Schools do not make scholars. A school may instruct a scholar. It may, on occasion, inspire one. But scholars are evolved from a combination of cultural factors quite beyond the powers of the school system to synthesize. When, as in the present period of general prosperity, the tendency is to give more young people more years of schooling, the consequence is that educational standards gradually are lowered. This is because it is necessary to adapt our curricula to the greater number, which inevitably will include some of lower mental capacity and a higher degree of resistance to learning.

The parents who long ago resolved that their children should have the "advantages" of which they themselves were perhaps partially deprived are to be commended. This is a determination we all can understand and one with which there is a high degree of empathy. Certainly in this modern age every child has a right to all the formal schooling it can absorb; every community, moreover, has the obligation to see that appropriate educational facilities are made available. This is a duty not only to the individual but to the community in toto, since it has and will continue to have imperative need for schooled brains.

The great misconception comes about in our bland acceptance of a belief that all young people are equally educable. They are not. There are tremendous differences in their capacities to absorb and assimilate knowledge. It is high time we ceased making ourselves and our offspring miserable in a wholly futile effort to pound more formal learning into a mind than that mind is capable of accepting.

Very often you will hear the wistful plaint from some person in later life, "I could have been a great actor [or dancer or vocalist] if my people had been able to give me advantages." This must be accepted as a rationalization for landing in the mire of mediocrity. Perhaps the individual in question had some aptitude for one of the arts; even talent, it may be. But by the law of averages it is preposterously unlikely the holding was much better than that. If fond parents had expended every nickel they could scrape together they might have been rewarded with a stock-company Bernhardt who would wind up as a wardrobe mistress, embittered because her meager talent (yclept "the system") could not take her to the top.

There is no warrant for what I am about to say. The statement cannot possibly be proved. Yet I believe it as implicitly as I believe anything in this world. Yes, I believe that when genius of a great order is given to a person anywhere, in any age, that genius must become manifest. It has no other course. For that is the nature of high genius. It must burn its way through any adverse circumstance to gain the light of recognition. It cannot be smothered; it cannot be thwarted; it has to come out.

Below the range of genius, but still significantly important, are the aptitudes and the talents. In every individual these evidences of cultural gifts should be encouraged and developed. They enrich the personality, add to the individual's capacity for creative appreciation, and the expression of these talents often affords pleasure to others.

Whether this treasured possession should lead to a vocation or an avocation is a matter for time and the individual to determine. The parent can do almost nothing beyond standing ready to lend a helping hand, a supporting arm when and where it is needed. Greatness in the arts is never attained through parental pressure.

As a parent you must accept the fact that not many Great Ones are born into the world in a generation. How many opera stars of great magnitude are needed in the modern world? How many first-rate concert pianists can find employment? In the entire United States today there are less than five hundred men and women making their living exclusively from the writing of novels for the conventional publishing trade. By simple mathematical calculation the likelihood that one of your brood is thus touched is not great. Yet young mothers in particular are disposed to look into a cradle at a future policeman or foreman of the sewer construction gang and see nothing less than a resplendent alderman.

Although the chance of great talent in your household is not great, it cannot be discounted. We must be mindful, too, that the creative arts increasingly call for those with strong, well-developed aptitudes but lesser talents. Consider the case of young Paul who at the age of eleven wrote an essay on the polar bear that won the admiration of his teacher and straightway convinced the lad's mother that she had a Hemingway on her hands. Well, possibly she has, but let us not grow overly emotional on the prospects. It is a long and lonely way from polar bear essays to Pulitzer prizes.

A great many things may happen in the intervening years. Paul may have a certain facility with words without the essential imagination or creative fire. Or he may lack the stamina, the vital energy constantly to slug his way forward toward perfection in his craft. This does not mean that Paul should give up writing. So long as working with words seems to be his bent he must be encouraged. Though he may never rival Hemingway he may yet become a first-rate producer in advertising, in radio or television, or in some other phase of the incredibly developing communications industry.

Now and again we encounter great love for one of the arts, along with relatively meager gifts. "Oh, Lord," chanted one of the medieval monks, "I bring Thee little talent, but a boundless love." Said a young girl I once knew, "Even though I spend my whole life as a candlebearer of the Queen in the third act I must be in the opera. It is all that matters to me." Such lives may be touched with tragedy, but to deny a devotion of that order is unthinkable. About all a parent can do in such a situation is to step aside—and pray.

Katharine Cornell used to tell a wonderfully warming story of a pair of young vaudeville hoofers in the old days, playing a split week at Peoria. On a cold, stormy winter night they crept from the stage door of the theater and made their way, shivering and shaking, to the curb, dreading the four-block walk to their shabby theatrical hotel. As they waited for the lights to change, a limousine drew up. In the rear seat they glimpsed a woman wrapped in costly furs and dripping with jewels. Beside her sat a gentleman in evening attire.

The little girl hoofer nudged a little closer to her companion, "Oh, honey," she chattered, "wouldn't it be wonderful to have things like that!"

"Yeah," sighed the boy, "yeah, it sure would." And then

he brightened visibly. "But of course you can't have everything. And remember, sweetheart, *they can't act!*"

There are others who take a more rational view of their talents. I knew a young tenor. He was good—very good. From early youth he had been set on music as a vocation. I lost track of him in his freshman year at college. When next we met he was a practicing physician in a Middle-western city. I asked him about the switch.

"Music is still my first love," he admitted, "but I finally had to face the realities. I was good, but I was not of the best. There always would be tenors by the tens and the hundreds to surpass me. In music I could look ahead only to a life of relative obscurity and erratic employment, winding up perhaps at the age of fifty selling tickets in a box office for attractions in which I could no longer participate. I thought it over long and carefully and decided that music as a profession was not for me. Of course," he concluded, "I sing in the bathtub. I sometimes warble on my round of calls. I belong to a small group called Medical Musicians who horse around a bit in their spare time. Once in a while we even make public appearances. Now and then I sing for a wedding or a funeral. I have my opportunities for self-expression. My life is far from barren, and I am well content. Of course, I'm not a great physician either," my young friend concluded, "but I am a good one, and I will get better as I grow older, and at the same time I am giving my family an increased measure of security."

So there you have two sides of a sometimes insoluble problem. A parent can only try to remember that in the final analysis career decisions are the responsibility of the child. It is his life, not yours, that is to be lived. He must try to do with his years those things that promise to yield him the greatest measure of enduring satisfaction. He doesn't have to be great. He doesn't have to be renowned. He doesn't even have to be notably successful. His sole obligation is to make the best and most rewarding life he can from the varied treasures with which nature has endowed him.

Bruce Barton, board chairman of the big Batten, Barton, Durstine and Osborn advertising agency, said to me a long time ago, "Some twenty or thirty years from now I want people to say of me, 'There goes old man Barton. He is the father of three children, all doing well.' I don't care," he concluded, "whether any one of the three is ever rich or famous. I don't care whether any honors or awards ever are heaped upon them. I seek for them only the boon of sound physical and mental health and happy, productive, satisfying lives."

It always has seemed to me that is about as much as any parent reasonably can ask.

Now we come again, after a long and circuitous route, to a consideration of the social theme. We have already seen that the social order has not crumbled, as some have predicted. We still have the families of hereditary wealth, although their number is greatly diminished and unwieldly personal fortunes are being syphoned off through foundations. Along with these are the persons who by breeding and accepted social challenges are ascendant. Then we have the very considerable number who by personal distinction demand recognition. These are the successful authors, the popular artists, the leaders in all the arts, and the foremost practitioners of the professions.

Finally, we come to the middle class, now swollen to prodigious numbers. Since, as we have seen, not too many of these families are going to get out of this category, no matter how much money papa makes, perhaps we should accord the wealthiest ones some sort of distinction, for whatever it may be worth. So we shall draw a line. Over on this side we have the Middle Class—Much Moola. Those on the other side of the line represent Middle Class—Modest Means.

Looking further, it is gratifying to observe that the grindingly, desperately poor, although still with us, are diminishing in number. Once our most numerous group in any metropolitan center, they now are reduced as a class to the misfits, the misanthropists, the chronic unemployables.

At first glance, except for the variations as noted, this looks much like the social setup we have had for a very long time. And yet under the surface a change is apparent—a very significant change. Within the past very few years we have seen an instinctive gathering of our intellectual forces. Gradually the abler men and women are being drawn to the centers of government, industry, the sciences. The eggheads are getting ready to run the world. Not the radicals. Not the impractical theorists. But the smartest men and women we can find anywhere. They are going to take over because all of a sudden things have just gotten too much for the dunderheads and blunderbusses. The world has grown too complex, too involved, too technical for mediocre men to meddle with.

There will be no wholesale revolution, no sensational house-cleaning. Slowly, imperceptibly we shall have to move in our better men for the very practical reason that no lesser breed can manage the modern world. Nor do we mean just a few good men heading up our giant operations. The need will be for good men—smarter men than we have had in the past—wherever responsibilities arise and decisions must be made.

This dominance of intellect in high places has not been apparent since the days of our founding fathers. Then the supreme challenge of independence brought forth our ablest men. They were fewer in number, more readily detected, and they fell naturally into positions of compatibility.

To be sure, we have since that time had strong men to guide us in our hours of pressing need. Most of them have been hampered and hamstrung by incompetents. Lincoln's first Cabinet was sorely spotted by political appointees, misfits and mediocrities. Teddy Roosevelt once petulantly observed that there was more deadwood in Washington than in the petrified forest.

No reader lacks personal instances in support of our position that men and women in high posts are not always fitted by mental endowment for the posts they hold. Our point is not made wholly, or even primarily, in respect to government. Men of very limited abilities too often coast into responsible posts in business and industry through seniority, inheritance, or perhaps a shrewd ability to make money without the accompanying qualities that count for sound management.

We could tolerate these second-rate administrators through the horse-and-buggy days, and even limped along with them through the automative age. Now we are in the jet era. And the second-raters are out. It isn't simply that they have failed to keep pace with the time. It goes deeper than that. Candidly, they don't have the mental capacity to run the modern world. That is an assignment reserved for our very best brains.

Already the change is discernible. Everywhere the smart ones are moving in. More and yet more will follow. The most promising intellects in America are under observation. On every important college campus scouts are looking for leaders.

Although their talents differ widely and they may travel a thousand varying routes, these able men and women have one attribute in common—excellence of intellect. Within the lifetime of your children they shall comprise yet another social order in America, the emerging aristocracy of our First-Class Minds.

VII

PEOPLE:

Resewing the Seams

WE NOW COME to a point where we shall digress to discuss some of the problems that confront your child in his relations with other peoples of the earth. They are not new problems. They have been with us for a very long time. Our generation—as well as the generations before us—has been disposed to shunt these problems aside or to limp along with inadequate improvisations. That will no longer do. These problems are going to erupt in full explosive force within the active lifetime of your children. They shall be obliged to deal with them. To rear a generation in ignorance of these issues, or in indifference to them, would be the utmost folly. Thus any forecast of the world your children shall inherit must take into account these situations with respect to the remainder of the human family.

Our first problem concerns population—the sheer number of mortals on the face of the earth.

Throughout the greater part of human history the monarchs and the merchants have conspired to sponsor propaganda for propagation. In all lands, in all ages, the production of people has been a primary concern.

The injunction to increase stands implicit in every enduring religion. Temporal spokesmen down the centuries have echoed the commandment to "multiply and replenish the earth." For a young world—a world in troubled transition—could inch its way onward only so long as there were people to shoulder the burdens. People to strengthen the sinews of state and foil the invader; people to fell the forests and till the soil; people to spend their strength and substance on a timeless treadmill; people to fertilize the earth for more people yet to come.

Despite these strong encouragements and admonitions, the course of the human species has on the whole been neither swift nor smooth. For uncounted centuries human life was repressed by plague and pestilence; by flood and famine; by untamed elements and savage marauders.

The average human life span at the height of the Roman Empire could hardly have been more than twenty-five years. For a very long time the rate did not greatly improve. Indeed, there were periods during the Middle Ages when our number was in decline; sizable areas where actual survival of the species was not infrequently at test.

It took mankind fifty centuries to reach a world total of one billion persons. This occurred about the year 1830. And then just look what happened. In another one hundred years—a single century—we had added a second billion. It is going to take just about thirty-five years to pile up our third billion. At this accelerated rate there are forecasters who go so far as to suggest that world population may pass six billions before the end of the twentieth century.

The problem, of course, is not so much the sheer number of people as it is their geographical distribution. Populations are increasing most rapidly in those blighted and backward countries where governments are clearly unable to meet the needs of the peoples they now have.

At first glance one may ask why, in our relative isolation of fifty-three persons per square mile, we should be directly concerned with the problems of a people whose population density is ten times greater than our own. The simple answer is that there are no longer any private rooms in the world hostelry. Or, to put it another way, we can no longer live in communities isolated from our neighbors by oceans, mountains or other barriers. Residing as we necessarily do "in the midst of everywhere," with no land more than a few hours away, a foreign ill, an alien hunger, becomes our constant concern. It is no longer solely or perhaps even primarily a matter of compassion. Our very freedom is involved in the action. If we do not help these people now to find some solution to their problem, complete disintegration is imminent. A meaningless, incoherent uprising of vast masses of inert humanity could result only in complete chaos. The inevitable consequence would be a succession of radical governments inimical to our interests and a constant threat to our security.

We have no more than fifty years left to master the art of human population control, declares Dr. John Rock, professor emeritus of gynecology at Harvard University. "Unless the birth rate is sufficiently cut within a short fifty years," he says, "the hungry and crowded peoples of the earth will rise in bestial strife."

Billions are vague and incomprehensible to most minds. Let us bring to you some figures that show a little more intimately—a little more humanly—what the problem really is.

The United Nations estimates that world population is growing by 5,400 every hour, or approximately 47 million a year. This, you understand, represents the net increase of births in excess of deaths.

An example of how this works out is demonstrated in Mexico, where the annual birth rate is 46 per thousand population (nearly three times the current Western European rate) while the death rate is 13. At this rate there could be 60 million Mexicans in twenty years, compared with the present 30 million.

No country can hope to keep pace in its resources with such rapid population increases. Thus it is estimated that half of the 90 million babies born this year will be undernourished.

With characteristic well-intentioned clumsiness, the white man is partially responsible for the present population plight. Throughout this century, and particularly during the period of the Second World War, we plunged into primitive countries bringing our new medical discoveries and vast improvements in sanitation. The consequence was that we cut death rates sensationally in many areas. Naturally, with no abatement in births, this has resulted in an imbalance that becomes more marked with the passing years.

Of course we have tried quite consistently and on the whole successfully to help these primitive peoples improve their natural resources. India affords an enlightening example of the consequences.

About ten years ago we began our intensive effort to aid India with her agricultural problem. Somewhat to the surprise of our agricultural experts the soil proved highly responsive. Lands that had produced only a meager crop of third-rate corn were soon yielding one hundred bushels to the acre of first-rate hybrid corn. Hens were laying five times as many eggs as formerly. Other developments were in proportion. A delighted Indian agricultural administrator, lecturing in the United States in 1957, reported that in a good crop year India could now come within 12 per cent of sustaining her own people.

Unhappily she has fallen behind since that time. I believe the present lack is somewhere in the range of 17 per cent. It is not that improved agricultural methods have failed to measure up. It is simply that here again the administrators have been unable to cope with the rising population.

Here again we are in some unwitting way partially responsible. For a generation we and our British cousins have been cleaning up India, vastly improving sanitary conditions, training local people for nurses and medical practitioners. As is always the case in primitive social orders, success was spectacular. People began living longer. Death rates went down. Meanwhile there was no letup in fecundity. The baby crop grew year by year.

What life was like in India before our "clean-up" program can hardly be imagined. J. Russell Smith, writing in *The World's Food Resources,* declared that even within this century human bones have been taken to the Indian fertilizer factories by the trainload because whole populations have perished and "not even the most distant kin of the dead remained on earth to bury them."

Granting that most of the backward countries can very materially increase their food production, that they might in time even raise enough to take care of a stable population, the catch is of course that populations do not remain stable. Such a project, even for a single small country, calls for capital far beyond the disposition of the United States or any other developed nation. It also calls for education, skill and management, none of which is presently available in the required proportions.

This will have to be taken a step at a time. The first essential step, obviously, is to find some way of reducing the birth rate. This isn't the matter of eugenics that comes up for periodic discussion in civilized social orders. It is an issue of stemming the senseless tide of humanity that continually engulfs and overwhelms a government more rapidly than remedial measures possibly can be taken.

It isn't that the people want these babies. Medical workers find primitive women pathetically eager to avoid the constant drains and strains of childbirth. They flock to social hygiene centers wherever and whenever they are set up. "But they are so abysmally ignorant," the workers say, "that it is all but impossible to reach them."

After three years on a single simple project, one medical missionary reported:

I think we are beginning to make a little progress with the younger women on our bead program. We devise strings of beads for the women who visit our clinics. These beads are related to the woman's menstrual period. We try very hard to impress the significance. White beads represent the "safe" days, the periods when a woman may have intercourse with her husband. The colored beads represent "danger" days or "baby" days, and a woman must then be on guard. As I say, I think some of the brighter ones are just beginning to get the idea. But it is a slow, tedious and uncertain course.

For fifty years, more or less, our medical missionaries, and those from other lands as well, have been prodding the men of science to get along with what, in the parlance of the profession, has been termed "the pill."

The pill as ideally conceived is a simple tablet, capable of inexpensive production in vast quantities, that will effectively curb the process of ovulation in females for a prescribed period, without producing permanent sterility or injury to any organ.

We now have that product.

These may well be the five most significant words in this volume. They promise to usher in an era that must result in profound changes throughout the greater area of the earth's surface. For the first time in human history man holds within his grasp the power to alter humanely the course of entire populations.

To be sure, the pill is not yet in a perfect state of development. The full measure of exultation must be slightly delayed. The pill is real enough. It contains recently discovered compounds, called steroids, that do unquestionably block ovulation. Experiments in the West Indies and in Puerto Rico, extending for as long as three years, demonstrate that the contraceptive will prevent pregnancy without setting up side effects. However, there are at the moment two obstacles. The pill must be taken daily to be effective. This is impracticable for primitive people who cannot be under constant surveillance. They cannot be depended upon to maintain regularity of dosage. Another point is that the tablets still are relatively expensive for widespread distribution.

It is the hope of all concerned that a new form of the product with more prolonged action will soon be available. Also, the prospect for economical synthesis of the pellet is said to be bright. The "breakthrough" may be expected at any time. Certainly it cannot be delayed many years.

Then, and only then, can we begin to do something about an overpopulated world that, at certain very sore spots, is threatening to come unsewed at the seams. At that happy moment we shall have the materials to start effectively resewing some of those seams. Any other form of aid to backward countries can be little more than transient relief.

VIII

PEOPLE:

Little Lily White
and the Raging Colored Sea

THE NOTION THAT a few hundred million white men could ever permanently subjugate colored persons of the world in an aggregate of two billion, is an idea so preposterous it could have occurred only to a white man.

Yet for a period of five hundred years—and probably for a much longer time—white men have been trying to do very much that sort of thing. Our earliest written records tell of their departure for, and sometimes of their return from, distant and colorful lands. Always these expeditions were made for purposes of conquest and plunder. Sometimes these expeditions gave a superficial appearance of profit. There were the usual evidences that all might see—precious jewels, strange new fabrics, queer birds and animals, tropical fruits, pungent herbs and spices. And not infrequently there were slaves—black, silent, sullen, and subjugated.

Oh, yes, there were more and more voices, as the years wore on, to attest the profits of foreign trade. Very few considered that it was not trade, in any equitable sense of the term. It was subjugation and/or slavery. Again and again, until the theme became threadbare with repetition, white men marched into a country and overran helpless colored peoples by force of arms. Systematically they drained a land of its natural resources, consistently giving the natives as little as practicable in return. And in the end leaving a legacy of disease, sullen resentment, and the smoldering determination for revenge.

The foreign trade was real enough. The profits it yielded were highly negotiable. It all made a very pleasant picture. One is not surprised to learn that Queen Victoria, in the late 1890's, observing a fleet of merchantmen moving in stately procession down the Thames, expressed the pious hope that a hundred years hence there would still be British vessels off garnering treasures from exotic foreign ports to enrich her subjects.

There is no record that the Queen expressed concern for the original owners of those treasures or took steps to see that they were properly compensated for the white man's confiscations.

After the sporadic adventurers came the colonists seeking to found their fortunes on purloined land. Always they came with the blessing and often at the behest of their monarch.

Yet if we reckon the colonial experiences of all the white men of all ages, setting the assets against the liabilities, there is grave doubt that any nation anywhere ever made a penny of profit from its colonials. With a few atypical exceptions, such as the North American continent and Australia, where there was space enough to assure every newcomer ample domain without abridging the rights of any native, each expedition carried the seeds of eventual failure in its cargo.[1]

---

[1] Even in the United States our treatment of backward peoples has not always been unassailable. There is a story in Washington that a committee was formed in 1958 to study broken treaties in which the United States had been a participant, the thought being that perhaps we could uncover some key to the production of more enduring documents. The committee was quietly disbanded in the spring of 1959. It was found that most of the treaties available for study bore references to the "Paleface President," and employed such terms as "Indian know white man talk straight, but sometimes bend in wind."

Those seeds might lie dormant for decades or for centuries. Some have not yet come to life. But sprout they must. For colonialism, as practiced by the white man, has been based on a creed of seizure and spoilage; a rule of might. Might does not win victories. It can only subdue victims.

We have but to look about us at the state of affairs in our world today. Everywhere colonialism is a decadent and dying practice. Observe how, within our generation, Britain moved almost eagerly to renounce its hold upon India. In South Africa the natives regain step by step their hold over the usurping white man. Ponder the difficulties of France in Algeria. Everywhere the story repeats: colonialism is dying out in the modern world. We shall witness its requiem in our century.

The death of colonialism is not its end. Wraiths from the distant past may walk the restless earth for yet another hundred years, spilling venom into the veins of men whose sires have not yet been conceived. That, in simple truth, is the modern burden of the white man, heavier by a hundredfold than the Kipling cross.

No one has any accurate statistics as to the relative ratio of white and colored men in the present world. No one possibly can have. There are no accurate census tabulations. Nor will there be in our lifetime. For great areas of the world's surface we have done no more than make shadowy estimates, and these are outdated before they can be put into print.

Then, too, a great deal depends upon one's definition of "white" and colored. There are all manner of tints representing varying degrees of pigmentation.

If our definition is to be restricted to the pure Caucasian strain, as found primarily in North America and in Western Europe and in limited numbers in other areas of the world, then the total of this group may well be under a billion. Against these must then be arrayed the colored peoples, ranging from the only slightly tinted Slavs to the Negroid.

It would, of course, be normal to rank the Slavs with our white group. We have separated them in our enumeration chiefly because they have separated themselves from us ideologically. In any struggle that may ensue for the survival of the Western world, the hand of the Slavic people, under domination of Russia, will be against us.

We should not, however, conclude from this that the Caucasian whites stand alone. They have firm friends among the tinted peoples of the earth. The significant point is that we need and must have more to offset the frantic evangelical fervor of the Russian and Chinese hordes when they go forth to plant the banner of Communism on foreign soils.

The question comes down to this in its naked realities: Can the white men, acting simply and in all sincerity, wipe out the stagnant, bitter memories of colonial brutality, mismanagement and malfeasance, in time to offset the Communist pleas that may fall seductively upon ears that have been too long attuned to the snap of a white man's whip? Are there enough hours left to win the credulity of the world's uncommitted billion? There *must* be time, else the fate of the human species, and more particularly the Caucasian segment of it, lies in the balance. Otherwise we shall view the spectacle of Little Lily White afloat on the Raging Colored Sea. It could be a story more grim than anything envisaged by the brothers Grimm. And, unhappily, not a fairy tale.

There was a time when we could rest secure in the belief that our technological superiority could keep us safe from any aggressive danger. No one would dare attack the Mighty West! Any threatening move would bring instant and complete disaster upon the enemy. In this belief we were schooled from infancy. Every observation appeared to uphold our opinion. Then came the quick, bitter years of disillusion and dismay; the realization that another power, pitted against us ideologically, must be viewed as a relentless opponent.

We may not encounter this foe in an atomic clash, but we must meet, inevitably, in economic battles as we clash for the good will and patronage of the world's uncommitted peoples.

If we lose these peoples we shall have lost the last war we ever shall have occasion to fight aggressively. It will not mean our sudden obliteration, our instant doom and downfall. We may be permitted to live along on our recollections. But the West definitely will be in decline. Even with the few friends we could muster on the fringes we could not hold our own against the battalions of color arrayed against us. In any such test the myth of white supremacy would fall from us like a rumpled garment. We would be revealed before the colored world merely as naked members of the human species, somewhat deficient in pigmentation.

IX

PEOPLE:

The Coming War of Wares

"WE WILL BURY YOU!" declared Soviet Premier Nikita S. Khrushchev. His reference was not to a military but to an economic funeral. Communist doctrine, of course, always has held that capitalism must fall of its own weight. Khrushchev has been trying with a sly little push here and there to hasten the course of Socialism in the wider world.

In an earlier chapter we quoted an American industrial executive, familiar with the Soviet structure, as saying that wherever in the world Russians proffer steel they also may be counted upon to sell Communism. The statement is sufficiently significant —and well enough documented—to warrant a repetition. It is one of the primary points that give such significance to the impending battles for world trade, or what we have termed the coming war of wares.

According to a statement issued by the United States State Department on June 15, 1958, the Soviet bloc in a period of five years had extended $1 billion in military and economic aid to fourteen "less developed" countries, while its trade with these countries expanded 70 per cent. That this trade is politically

motivated is of course unquestioned. It is one of the more sober-
ing aspects of the war of wares.

These figures, although impressive, are not large in comparison with foreign operations of the United States for a comparable
period. Inevitably, therefore, the question arises as to why the
West, which carries the major part of the burden of developing
the backward areas of the earth, should receive so little recognition in comparison with the rather trivial contributions of the
Soviet Union. In this connection a writer in the London *Observer,* in the autumn of 1958, hazarded this opinion:

"One of the reasons why the Soviet's tiny trickle of aid to the
under-developed countries has been such a propaganda success
is that they represent it as a fraternal gift from a pioneer and
partner in the great struggle of taming nature. Our aid too often
seems only the patronage of the rich to the poor."

To put it another way, Russian propagandists have contrived
to surround her meager alms with some of the significance of
the widow's mite. While boasting to the West of vast industrial
gains, the Soviet Union is scrupulously careful in its benefactions
to preserve an identity with the "have-not" nations. Moreover,
she loses no opportunity to remind her Eastern neighbors that
"we are all Asians together."

Finally, of course, Russians employ the reiterative philosophy
of the old Negro preacher who explained, "First, I tells them
what I is goin' to tell 'em. Then I tells 'em. An' finally I tells
'em what I has done told 'em."

Each individual parcel of Russian aid is heralded in antici-
pation, again upon realization, and in retrospect as frequently as
occasion may offer. Thus the sum total of Russian benefactions
is made to appear rather more consequential than it really is.

The West is not trying to outdo the Russians in this game of
artifice but to present its infinitely more substantial contributions
for precisely what they are: sound business investments that will
bring an increased measure of prosperity to all concerned without

the stigma of alms. People may not exactly love a banker, but they respect him and are proud to be associated in his endeavors.

The significant point is that the size of the Soviet Union's benefactions is carefully screened from the people at home. They do not have the remotest idea of what is being spent for propaganda purposes. This probably minimizes the unrest that more is not being spent to improve conditions of the Russian people.

It is now more than thirty years since Russia, forming her first "five-year plan," coined the slogan, "Surpass America!" Except for a wartime interlude, this objective has been kept in the foreground of Russian planning. It is only in a comparatively recent period that Party Chief Khrushchev has established a definite date for the objective. He now forecasts that the Soviet Union will be the world's No. 1 industrial nation "within a space of fifteen years."

Is this an idle boast, or does the proposal have some solid substance? Reviewing the situation realistically, it must be admitted that the Soviet has two essentials for industrial supremacy— population and resources. What she can and will do with these assets remains a question for the future. Other peoples before Russia have possessed both factors and failed to fuse them effectively. On the other hand, Great Britain, in her heyday, stood a notable exception. She achieved industrial dominance despite acute limitations of population and natural resources.

What, precisely, are the treasures of the Soviet Union? They are admittedly impressive. F. Antropov, minister of geology and subterranean resources, estimates that the Soviet Union has 41 per cent of the world's known reserves of iron ore (some of it running as high as 60 per cent iron content); 60 per cent of the coal and 88 per cent of the manganese. There is gold in some substantial volume. And geologists speak favorably of the vast diamond fields in Yakutia. Moreover, the Soviet is said to hold a premier position in deposits of copper, lead, zinc, nickel, bauxite, wolfram, mercury, mica, titanium, molybdenum, tin and uranium. Finally, the Soviet Union has great stores of oil, although it is not so accessible as resources in other areas.

It must be said in conclusion that the full exploitation of resources demands resourcefulness. Russia has the metal. Does she possess the mettle? She has yet to demonstrate an ability, to master mass production techniques.

For an account of how Russia has been doing in production, let us turn to the records. In the five-year period from 1952 to 1957, industrial production in the Soviet Union rose 12.7 per cent, while in the United States comparable production had gone up only 4.1 per cent in the same period.

True, Russia has yet a long way to go before she can compete with us quantitatively. The significant point is that Soviet industrial production is ascendant. Her rate of growth is three times greater than our own. That is the sort of thing that permits tireless tortoises to win races over heedless hares.

It is pointed out, too, that Russia, because of her greater population, will need production far greater than our own totals in order to provide her peoples with something approaching our standards of living. The common assumption is that these goals must be attained before Russia is concerned over foreign markets. This is a totally fallacious point of view. A dictatorship can set standards at whatever point it wishes, exporting any and all production above these minimums. Russia has clearly indicated her intention of following this course.

What is perhaps equally to the point is that Russia need not wait until she has attained full equality with other producers to become a very troublesome competitor. She is indeed in that position already. She can demoralize a number of raw material markets when she elects to do so. In April of 1958 a two-cent reduction in aluminum was directly traceable to the Soviet Union. They undercut the established market and other nations had to meet the competition.

In August of that year the Soviet Union elected to dump 17,000 tons of tin on the world market, at the worst possible strategic moment, when the industry was already reeling from the effects of depression. The blow all but wrecked the vast capitalistic interests in Malaya, where the bulk of the world's tin actually is produced. Normally Russia's relatively light holdings would have been of no consequence. It was simply a matter of timing.

We have given here two practical demonstrations of how a socialized government monopoly, using a basic commodity as an economic-political tool, can work its will. Many similar instances could be revealed.

Right now Russian oil tankers are steaming up the River Plate to discharge their cargo at Buenos Aires. They represent installments on a million tons of crude that Russia has promised Argentina. No, she really hasn't the oil to spare, but it is part of a long-range policy. For Russia wants Argentine wool, linseed oil, tallow, etc. She will find the oil somewhere. Tomorrow there will be more. Meanwhile she has stolen a customer from under the nose of Uncle Sam. Allen Dulles, head of the Central Intelligence Agency, has warned that by 1972 the Soviet plans to produce as much crude oil as we in the United States do today. On such a basis they could perhaps export two million barrels a day. So they are out now looking for tomorrow's buyers.

What is not clearly understood in a capitalistic country is that our Socialist neighbors have no real concern with cost, in a normal production sense. There are no entrepreneurs to satisfy. Since everything belongs to the government and all revenue goes eventually to the government, they can dump a parcel here or there, wherever it may do the most damage, at any price one may fancy. It can be cruel competition for private capitalistic business.

Certainly we can erect trade barriers to keep Soviet commodities from our shores. But that is now a very small part of the problem. Great opportunities of the next quarter century lie in serving the growing needs of a wider world. Since Western Europe has now become largely self-sustaining, and is in many areas an active exporter, we must look to the backward countries for our trade. Our future lies not only in supplying the basic needs of these people but also in the process gaining their loyalty and active support for the principles of freedom. At the same time we must teach them how to evaluate and to develop their natural resources; how to operate such limited industries as they are able to keep going. All this we must do with a simple integrity and with a basic appreciation for the dignity of these natives as members of the human family.

All this is a good deal to expect. It is a great deal more than any exploiter of a foreign land ever has done in the past. However, it is the one chance we have to win the uncommitted colored peoples of the world to the ways of freedom and capitalistic enterprise. The odds are not encouraging. But we'll have to play out the hand as it is dealt. There is no other course.

These things we must do most assuredly without any wholesale attempts at Christian conversion. So long as Communists are trying to foster a new ethical concept along with their commodities, they are at a disadvantage. Let us not further complicate the situation with the technique of the package deal. Rather we should concentrate on the simple process of bringing in the things people need and taking out the things they have in abundance. Always operating at a fair profit for all concerned.

Let Christianity come as a natural consequence of following the pattern of our lives. Right now we can do more by example to make good Methodists, Baptists or Roman Catholics than in any other way. Asked to make a drastic fundamental change in their way of life, people naturally are going to be suspicious, antagonistic. Revolutions in thought are the most difficult to achieve. So let us not hasten to bring the Cross to a people who, in the past, have been too bitterly experienced in the double-cross.

It should hardly be necessary to add at this point that the Soviet Union, although by far our most serious problem, isn't the only group that will give us concern in the coming War of Wares. Europe is about to become a stiffer competitor. The postwar recovery is now pretty well achieved. Lots of fine, new machinery is now functioning. The old aggressiveness is apparent. You have already observed what has happened in the foreign invasion of the American automobile market.

The "Common Market" of Europe, of which you have heard a great deal, is developing rapidly. It is now operating smoothly and should be in high gear within five years. Leading nations of Western Europe are in the pool, working to abolish their own trade barriers, making a mass market within themselves, and uniting for large-scale trade abroad.

One incidental consequence of this industrial renaissance abroad is that a number of United States firms, instead of expanding in Europe, are contracting with European factors to manufacture their wares under license. Some also will distribute. It may work out a good deal cheaper. Europeans have the "economy knack." Only recently Kenneth Headlam-Morley, secretary of the British Iron and Steel Institute, pointed out to members of the American Society for Metals that Britain should consistently produce for less than America since, for one thing, wage rates are only about a third of those prevailing here.

Lower wage rates abroad have of course always been a sore topic with American producers. At the moment there certainly is no dearth of low-priced specialty items bearing foreign labels. True enough, the quality is rarely much to boast of, but the prices often are sensationally low.

Just recently a United States Marine officer of my acquaintance was whiling away a bit of time in a Washington gift shop. His eye was caught by a bronze paperweight depicting the familiar scene of Marines raising the United States flag at Iwo Jima, after routing the Japanese. Idly turning over the souvenir the

Marine officer was somewhat nonplused to note the label, "Made in Japan."

We have now considered three grave problems in relation to the lives of your children. These are not theoretical problems. Nor are they mere possible eventualities. The problems exist. There can be no possible issue on that point. We march steadily toward them every day of our lives. As said before, they will erupt explosively within a few years. One is perhaps more imminent than another. None can be pushed aside beyond the final quarter of our century. Which means, of course, that many of us, along with our offspring, will be embroiled in final solutions.

First, you will remember, I presented the problem of populations increasing more rapidly in backward countries than the facilities of established government can provide for them. I suggested as the only practicable remedy the wholesale scotching of fecundity until the human family in those areas of the world can be brought to manageable proportions.

As the only alternative action, I suggested inert and almost incoherent masses of humanity rising in senseless, bestial desperation against any established government that symbolizes their frenzy at inaction.

As a second problem, I brought to your attention the present danger that a dying colonialism may be leaving in the world such rancor and venom as to make impracticable the sincere efforts of fairly disposed white men to bring peace, prosperity and higher standards of living to millions who exist in primitive squalor.

Although this is a recognized danger, we have no alternative but to make the effort, and to do it now, before the forces of Communism move in to fill a void with their superficially persuasive doctrines.

Finally, I pointed out to you the inevitability of the coming War of Wares when, roughly, the Communist nations will be arrayed against the forces of enterprise in a gigantic struggle for ideas as well as inventories, for the minds of men as well as mere money.

Admittedly, none of these problems stands in ready solution. There is perhaps not a great deal that one individual can do about them, no matter how earnestly he may feel. We, nevertheless, present no apology for the intrusion. Not to know about these problems—not to be fully informed as to their causes and consequences—is the utmost folly.

Once, many years ago, a quiet college professor whom I knew well, set aside a good deal of time to discuss with his pupils a sociological problem to which he confessed quite candidly he could see no present remedy.

"If nothing can be done," asked an impatient student, "why have you taken up our time? What do you expect us to do?"

"Just be aware of the problem," said the professor quietly. "Just be aware of it."

Just being aware of a problem can make a tremendous difference. A citizenry fully informed on the issues—and on the consequences of inaction—is very likely to have a responsive representation.

X   THE DWINDLING FAMILY:

A Long-Range Trend

OBVIOUSLY WE CANNOT say that your children will produce fewer offspring than you produced. That gets us into the realm of fortunetelling or necromancy. We can say that in a hundred households—or in a thousand households—the total number of children produced by a rising generation is likely to be somewhat less than the total of the generation preceding.

We can say this with considerable assurance because our knowledge is based on trends of long duration. And trends, unlike fashions, fads and foibles, are not subject to rapid changes. For a much longer period than there are accurate statistics to support our position, women of childbearing age have been tending, in the aggregate, to reduce the number of their children. They have done this as living standards improved and the science of medicine lowered the mortality rate of infants.

Even in the Western world, as recently as the days of our great-great-grandparents, mortality records were shocking. Lord Astor wrote that in the time of John Wesley (who, incidentally, was his mother's fifteenth child) less than twenty-five in every one hundred children lived to see a fifth birthday. In colonial

America, even though founded on Europe's younger and more vigorous stock, the record was little if any better. Large families were everywhere considered a matter of common prudence, in order that a few might reach maturity to provide for rapidly aging parents.

You cannot place your finger upon a specific date and say, "At this point the large family became an economic liability rather than an asset." It was a gradual process of evolution, integrated with our transition from an agricultural to an industrial people; from a rural to an urban society.

Even after people began faintly to suspect that unbridled fecundity had its perils, and its price, elders pursued the placative technique. "God never sends mouths without sending meat," William Cobbett, the English pamphleteer, assured a young farmer who had made anxious inquiry as to the number of offspring he should father. Cobbett, it may be said parenthetically, had seven young mouths to feed, and the provision problem was not infrequently a major concern.

It is beyond our province to discuss the ethics of birth control. We are concerned solely with its sociological consequences and probable potential in relation to population trends. The family-limitation idea received earlier and wider acceptance in Europe, and particularly in England, than in America. This is to be expected, since population pressures and limited agricultural areas forced a greater degree of urban industrialization. Birth control certainly was in practice, stealthily but effectively, in England by 1850. The use of contraceptives was publicly advocated in England as early as 1877 by Charles Bradlaugh and Annie Besant. They were prosecuted for selling a pamphlet called *The Fruits of Philosophy.* The resulting publicity gave the movement quite a boost and led to the establishment of the Malthusian League (a move which the pious clergyman Thomas Robert Malthus could hardly have approved). Although directing attention to the perils of overpopulation in his famous *Essay*

on the Principle of Population, Malthus advocated late marriage
and sexual continence as the ethical means of control.

By 1924 J. Swinburne, a British consulting engineer, was able
to report:

> For about seventy years the limitation of families has
> been practiced. It began in the middle classes and spread
> both up and down; and it will gradually extend until it
> changes the whole of the relations of society. The limitation
> of offspring and the means to that end form the greatest dis-
> covery man has ever made. But no one knows the discoverer,
> and such matters are mentioned only with bated breath.

A few years later another British writer observed that "birth-
control is more nearly universal in our Western civilization than
the bath-tub or the telephone."

In America we have the rather unusual situation of a practice
well established and quite widely accepted before the pioneer
agitator came upon the scene. That pioneer was, of course, Margaret Sanger, a nurse by profession; a mother "by deliberate
intent." It was Mrs. Sanger, apparently, who first used the term
"birth control," in 1914. She published her philosophy of family
limitation in a monthly magazine, the *Woman Rebel.* In 1915
she was indicted for sending pleas for birth control through the
mails. Persisting against considerable opposition, she organized
the first American Birth Control Conference in New York in
1921 and subsequently became the first president of the American
Birth Control League, now known as the Planned Parenthood
Federation of America, Inc.

On the whole our attitude toward population trends in the
United States has been emotional rather than realistic. Around
the turn of the twentieth century extinction of the species was
freely predicted by alarmists on every hand. This hysteria was
considerably abetted by President Theodore Roosevelt, who wrote

and talked voluminously on the theme of "race suicide"—a term
which he did not originate but which became closely associated
with him. During this period Mr. Roosevelt, in his campaign for
larger families, wrote scores of congratulatory letters to parents
of numerous offspring implying, as one journalist put it, that
"the nearer Americans approach the physical status of rabbits,
the more patriotic they become."

More recently in our national history, following a decade of
rising birth rates, commonly characterized as our "baby binge,"
the discussions have taken on a somewhat Malthusian dolor.
Public prints feature articles on the disturbing rise in population.
There are frequent forums to question whether the race is out-
running its resources.

These two extreme, and violently contradictory, points of view
demonstrate rather graphically the American tendency to jump
to conclusions on superficial evidence.

An obvious reason for this increase in births is that the period
cited embraces the early postwar years—a time when postponed
marriages were being consummated. An increase in marriages
naturally increases the birth rate. But here, also, we enter a realm
of psychology that transcends mere mathematics.

Marriages postponed by war, and involving a prolonged sepa-
ration of the sexes, are more fruitful—and more rapidly fruitful
—than those consummated in normal course. The soldier in his
trench and the maiden waiting for him at home turn their
thoughts to family formation. When finally they are united there
seems to be a compulsive urge to compensate for precious lost
years.

Moreover, it must be realized that periods of war and great
economic stress have a marked effect on established households.
In parlous and unstable times births are postponed. When parents
experience a greater feeling of security these "postponed" children
are brought into the world. We see this manifested in the remarkable number of second, third, and even fourth children born

into established households in the ten years under discussion. If we were to judge solely by superficial evidence over a limited period, we should have to conclude that the larger family unit is again ascendant. Some predictions to that effect have been made in the recent past. Such a course would be in strong contrast to established, long-range trends. For various reasons responsible demographers are disposed to view this increase as transient.

For another possible factor contributing to the increased birth rate we shall have to go back a generation to a time when the one-child household was becoming prevalent. These solitary children, it is reasonable to assume, may have suffered from what might be termed a "sibling syndrome"—a complicated and exaggerated sense of loss from the absence of brothers and sisters. A natural reaction from such a condition would be the firm resolution to have a "houseful of kids." How many solitary children do you know who have themselves begat but a single child?

Nor can we overlook in our analysis the imitative factor. When larger families become the "fashion," so to speak, the influence upon those who move in a particular social circle cannot be lightly discounted. If Eloise and Horace have a second, or a third, child, Lucille and Marvin will take note. Presently we may anticipate little feet pattering through the subconscious.

This imitative factor is especially potent within the family circle. Sisters have a strong tendency to "even up" their households. If Barbara's three-year-old has been slightly displaced in the affectionate regard of fond grandparents by the arrival of Isobel's second baby, Barbara may be expected to take steps. Ceres, the goddess of fertility, is sometimes motivated by vexation.

A point worth noting is that the principals in a majority of these postponed marriages had substantial cash reserves. They were setting up housekeeping at a time of great industrial activity with prevailing high wages. Coupled with this, we must consider that the pent-up consumer demand resulting from commodity shortages during the course of World War II and the Korean police action resulted in a continuing scarcity of durables. The newlyweds had limited opportunities to spend their savings. It was an atmosphere calculated to stimulate propagation. This is illustrated by a facetious but believable anecdote of the period. A young couple were undecided as to whether they should acquire a new car or a baby. "We finally decided on a baby," said the wife brightly. "We could get quicker delivery."

This story brings up a pertinent point which we may digress momentarily to discuss. It concerns the constant conflict between our procreative instincts and our yearning for comforts, luxuries and social status.

We said in an earlier chapter, you will recall, that populations are kept in check when standards of living increase more rapidly than the wealth of nations. Reduced to an individual level, we may say as a generality that the size of a family diminishes in relation to its economic and social advancement. It is almost axiomatic in our society that the banker has fewer offspring than the barber. The banker may say that this is because he has a better developed sense of social responsibility. He and his spouse have elected to bring into the world only as many children as they can clothe, educate and properly supervise. This is a rational conclusion and in some degree a valid one. It also serves as a convenient cloak for our subtler and more impelling instincts of acquisitiveness and social advancement. With six children, rather than three, we could not afford a second automobile in the garage. Membership in the country club would be beyond our reach. And we should find ourselves lagging behind the Jones family—our undeclared but nevertheless effective social arbiters.

It should be noted that, while the barber may have more children than the banker, at the same time he probably has fewer than his sire, indicating that he also has become in some degree cognizant of social pressures.

This thesis that birth rates are adversely affected by our increasing material desires is by no means a new idea in the world.

It has long been observed that the lowest birth rates are found in the highly civilized, urbanized areas of the earth. "Society replenishes itself from its lower levels and dies off at the top."

More than a century ago the French economist Bastiat expressed the hope that workmen's standards of living would continue to rise "so that their numbers shall increase less rapidly."

In 1903 a father of four, writing anonymously in a journal of opinion to oppose Theodore Roosevelt's argument for larger families, made, for that period, an uncommonly frank admission:

> If a time should come when we had to give up our present standard of living, I should consider it perhaps the most serious day of my life. The thing that would most probably threaten such an event would be the arrival of, say, two more children. I am a fond father, but I say candidly that I want no further off-spring.
>
> Some may think this an ignoble statement, but it is true of almost every family of which I have personal acquaintance.

Thirty years later we find Carr-Saunders, the renowned British authority on populations, bringing up pretty much the same ideas but presenting them as an accepted commonplace:

> The small family fits in, not only with the enduring wishes of the mother, but also with the new mode of life. The last sixty years have seen an immense increase in leisure time, and a still greater increase in facilities for increasing that leisure; and children are impediments to those who wish to avail themselves of these facilities. In relation to making a living, children are now seldom a help and often an encumbrance. Finally, the effort to rise in the social scale may well be frustrated by a large family.[1]

[1] A. M. Carr-Saunders, *The Population Problem* (Oxford University Press).

"As wealth increases," concluded Nassau William Senior, the nineteenth-century economist, "what were the luxuries of one generation become the decencies of their successors."

Since it has been reliably estimated that the number of these "decencies," or common necessities, has more than tripled since the turn of the twentieth century, the reasons for family limitation become starkly apparent.

The forces that made for abnormal population increase in the years from 1947 through 1956 have about run their course. The birth rate began a decline in November, 1957—too early for the business recession to have been much of a restraining force. Regardless of economic conditions the trend will now be downward for a period of several years. This condition is readily understandable.

Those couples who married in the early postwar years have now, generally speaking, established their families. We have coming to maturity and marriage a generation born in the late-depression and early-war years. Since the "baby crop" was at a markedly low rate during that period, these couples are reduced in number. We may consequently expect a decline in what is termed the "crude" birth rate, which is based on total population.

This illustrates the fallacy of placing too much reliance on superficial statistics. Obviously the crude birth rate can be highly deceptive during periods when there are marked changes in the structure of a population. In the long run the growth of a people will depend (excluding immigration) upon the rate at which women of childbearing age are producing offspring. This is known as the adjusted (sometimes the "refined" or "true") birth rate. Let us, therefore, examine developments in that area.

Here we run into some difficulty in our endeavor to trace a long-range trend. Persons beyond the age of sixty, seeking birth certificates for passports, frequently are surprised to learn that no official record of birth is available. In many sections of this country accurate statistics were not available until well into the twentieth century. However, we have had a decennial census since 1790. This gives us an accounting of population in various age groups. By studying these records, along with known mortality rates for infants, demographers can come up with some pretty accurate summations.

In the year 1800 we deduce that a thousand women of child-bearing age (15 through 44) must have produced approximately 278 offspring. By 1850 the figure had dropped to 194. In 1900 the rate stood at 130, less than half the production of 1800. It was during this period that cries of "race suicide" became strident. Many sociologists expressed genuine concern. By 1930 the rate —now completely documented, of course—stood at 87 babies for each thousand women of childbearing age. The reproduction rate in the generation since 1930 has been erratic. During the depression years it sank below the replenishment level. Until very recently there has been an ascendant trend, for reasons just discussed. The crude birth rate—and possibly the adjusted rate as well—will decline for a relatively brief period. Then, as children born since 1945 mature and marry—even though propagation continues the long-range trend of moderate decrease, as we anticipate that it will—we may expect rather substantial population gains. Eventually, however, as a larger segment of the total population attains an age above the reproductive level, the burden upon the producers to sustain a continuous net increase will become intolerable.

It was this basic situation that led Dr. Louis I. Dublin, in 1930, to predict that the United States would reach a stationary population in 1970 of approximately 150 million persons. We are now 25 million above that estimate, with another decade to go. And the "leveling off" period has been extended to perhaps the first quarter of the next century.

Dr. Dublin, at that time chief statistician for the Metropolitan Life Insurance Company, was one of our foremost authorities on population. From the data then available his conclusions were tenable. What he could not foresee was the exhilarating effect on population growth of our amazing progress in reducing infant mortality. When you save the life of a middle-aged person you merely add a single unit to the population for a limited span of years. With an infant the story is dramatically different. The child matures, marries, reproduces. The children of that union in turn multiply.

Our population growth for a generation has been materially affected by the fact that we have shown a steady decrease in infant mortality. We cannot count on future improvement to offset any possible, or probable, reduction in the birth rate.

This leaves us only the prospect of increasing the longevity of our adult citizens. This we shall discuss in a subsequent chapter. The outlook is less promising than most persons imagine.

XI   THE WORKING WIFE:

A Vanishing Social Stigma

THERE STILL ARE males in our populace who persistently proclaim that woman's place is in the home. In periods of depression they complain that women should relinquish their jobs "to men who really need them."

If these males should take a more realistic look at the modern world, they would be compelled to adopt a more perceptive attitude. The simple truth is that women have only incidentally and to a minor degree usurped the jobs of men. They have made places for themselves in the economic structure which they fill with distinction and efficiency; places which they haven't the slightest intention of surrendering and from which we really have no wish to displace them.

We scarcely need the reminder that this is an attitude of relatively recent cultures. Middle-aged persons can recall when "the woman who worked" outside her home was considered an unfortunate creature deserving of our special commiseration. She was likely to be either a left-on-the-limb spinster, a widow, or a wife whose husband was "on the drink" or otherwise incapable of providing for his household.

The wife of a sober, industrious, although perhaps not notably successful, man who sought to supplement the family income by venturing into "public work" (except possibly schoolteaching) was certain to be criticized for bringing disgrace upon her helpmate; for confessing openly to the world that he was incapable of supporting his brood. The deplorable state of the family might in itself be an eloquent proclamation of failure. But no matter, the wife always must pretend that papa's pittance was ample to provide soup, shoes and schoolbooks for one and all. To work for wages was, for the married woman (even the childless woman), a last desperate resort. It brought humiliation to her husband, and to herself a social stigma not lightly erased.

All that is virtually a thing of the past. No modern wife who wants a public job gives more than a passing thought to the reactions of friends and neighbors. Who cares? And why should they? Probably most of them are working anyway, or will be sooner or later. A wife working for wages no longer signifies that the husband is a failure. On every hand there are too many examples of signally successful men whose wives punch time clocks.

They may punch these time clocks for a variety of reasons. And not infrequently a number of reasons may motivate a woman in a given situation. Sometimes women work for wages because they are bored; because they want money for a new home or for certain extra luxuries; because they demand the stimuli of outside contacts. Most frequently of all they work because the family needs the money. With children of school age, the wife and mother in a modern, well-managed home has time on her hands. She has a choice of spending it in more or less inconsequential ways or of concentrating on a desired objective, and thus attaining the means of a college education for son or daughter or a somewhat higher standard of living for the household. That she so often elects to get a job is a tribute to her common sense and recognition of values.

When the first telephone switchboard was installed in New Haven, Connecticut, a little more than seventy-five years ago, the operators were men. Their voices proved harsh; their manners not well adapted to expediting the service. So, almost at once, the telephone companies began looking around for women who could be trained to operate switchboards. So much more acceptable were the women that there has never been a serious question since of their virtual monopoly in this branch of telephony. Today the hundreds of thousands of women employed in this segment of the communications industry is impressive proof that women have earned a permanent place for themselves in a wider world.

And so it has been in our business offices and mercantile establishments. Women have moved in not to displace men but to supplement them. They interview callers with tact and courtesy, shielding busy men from needless interruptions; they tap the typewriter, file the letters, make innumerable telephone calls, and on top of everything else remind the boss to take his ten-o'clock tranquilizer.

All this reveals our old friend, woman, in only a slightly differing role. The contention that even in the old days a woman's interests were limited to children, church and kitchen is palpably false. The woman who never earned a penny outside her home still, with rare skill, followed a dozen crafts. She had to be seamstress, milliner, cobbler and carpenter, merely to get the day's work done. Now things have simmered down a bit. The "children's hour" no longer extends from dawn to dark. Mother begins again to know the meaning of "spare time." Some of this time she resolves to turn to profit. What she has done, in simple truth, more often than not, is to move her workshop into the office. There she is carrying on pretty much the same versatile operation, and getting well paid for it. And there is the final inducement: she is evading daytime TV!

Modern women are marrying earlier, having their children at an earlier age. Today by the time a woman reaches her middle thirties her children no longer require constant supervision. It is at about that time she would do well to sit down and meditate with herself in this manner:

"I am now thirty-five years of age. By the law of probabilities I'll be around here for another thirty-five years—the median age for females now being seventy-two. So—what am I going to do with the rest of my life? Thirty-five perfectly good years—as long again as I have lived up to the present moment. That's too much time to fritter away. I had better find me something to do."

Whether that "something to do" is in the commercial area or in the realm of social service does not at the moment especially concern us. The significant point is that the woman of today has an opportunity such as has never before been offered to women. The adjustment of women to this era in which careers and children go hand in hand is in some degree an expression of the millennium. That era is of course only beginning. The maturing generation can't quite realize what is happening. It is your children, as young parents, who will be faced with the complete realization of this new freedom.

All the evidence at hand seems to indicate that increasingly in the future young matrons will choose commercial careers, as against activities in civic enterprises that yield no personal profit. It is very largely a matter of that old debil standard of living. *Newsweek,* a year or so ago, made the assertion that the fate of America's high standard of living now rests in the well-manicured hands and well-coifed heads of its women.

Actually it comes down to a matter of simple arithmetic. To support our rising standard of living, the experts tell us, we shall have to boost gross national production about 25 per cent, or say another billion dollars, by 1965. But even with all the automation we can muster that job will require ten million new workers. Since there is no such reservoir of male labor, at least half the number, or five million, will have to be women.

As we have seen, the modern economic world simply couldn't function without women. They have integrated themselves into the entire structure. Even those of us closest to the scene must express surprise at the extent to which women have come to perform services of a specialized nature, where they have made themselves well-nigh indispensable.

Speaking before a meeting of the National Manpower Council in Washington, in the fall of 1957, James P. Mitchell, as Secretary of Labor, gave an estimate of twenty-eight million as the female labor force at that time. Two years earlier, in 1955, he had estimated that forty-six out of one hundred women over fourteen years of age found employment outside the home at some time during the year. The Secretary freely estimated that the figure would exceed 50 per cent by 1965.

In other words, what we are saying is that nearly one half of the mature women of this country, quite apart from age or marital status, find some gainful employment during the year. (Less than half of them, we may add, work 52 weeks a year.) When you consider the millions of women obviously tied to their homes with small children, the mature matron who does not at some time turn her hand to a paying job would appear to be an exception.

So now what can we contemplate for your married daughters and your daughters-in-law half a generation hence? The prospect that these young matrons will work outside the home "until the babies come" is rather better than at the moment. Certainly we can anticipate no diminution in the burdens thrust upon the householder. What with inflation and increased taxation they will tend to grow heavier. That second check will be sorely needed, especially during the early formative years while a young man is establishing himself in the business world. The "working wife" will be accepted almost as a matter of course.

Who will do the housework?

It may not come as good news to the men but a more equitable division of domestic labor will come about almost automatically. When a wife puts in the same number of hours in office or shop as the husband—and often contributes almost as much to the family fund—then a split of the necessary homework is clearly indicated. Man's innate sense of fairness will assert itself and he may be expected to pitch in with vacuum cleaner and dust mop. Wise mothers should begin now giving young sons some preliminary training. Break down his prejudice against household chores as "woman's work" and you may have taken a longer step than you realize toward saving your son's marriage.

It should be hardly necessary to observe that the prospects for "hired help" are not bright and cannot be expected to improve.

"There is no servant problem in this country," declares a matron of my acquaintance. "The problem has not been solved; it has been dissolved. There are no servants, ergo no servant problem."

This is the extreme pessimistic view. There *are* servants available. And there are determined householders in pursuit of them. To serve our 48,785,000 households there are, according to the most recent United States Bureau of Census estimate, some 2,121,000 private household workers of both sexes.

Candidly, no informed person accepts the statistic. The classification is a notorious catchall for persons of dubious occupation or no occupation at all. The Census Bureau is, after all, an enumerative rather than an investigative branch of government. A widely experienced employment agent estimates there are not more than a million bona fide female domestic servants available for private employment in the entire nation. And he adds dourly that there will be less than half that number available twenty years hence.

Servants, as we have known them, will be virtually extinct in another twenty-five years. This is a fact of life. Unpalatable as it may be, we must accept it. A decade ago the New York State Department of Labor made a survey of former domestics who had turned to the factories during the war years. Only one in seventy-three expressed any desire to return to their former occupation. Now, ten years later, we know even more conclusively that the maids are not coming back to the maisons. There is no new reservoir of unskilled labor upon which to draw.

A generation ago millions of men and women performed menial services, not because they were limited in ability-potential but primarily because they lacked the education and training to rise to higher estate. These uneducated or ill-educated menials are disappearing. Their children will not be thus handicapped. We are educating our younger generations out of drudgery. In this condition we may discern the inevitable doom of historic servitude.

It is sometimes suggested that we might solve our servant problem as we solved it a century ago—by opening our gates to immigration. There is in this proposal a certain deceptive plausibility. Let us examine the proposal more closely.

First, we'd have to assume a willingness of government authorities to admit aliens in substantial number. Of this there certainly is no present indication. We were unable, in a recent session of Congress, to amend our restrictive legislation even to a point of letting in a few thousand additional victims of the Hungarian revolution.

There must also be a presumption of willingness on the part of other nations to permit a drainage of their populations. This is a most unrealistic conclusion. Conditions today in no sense parallel those obtaining in 1850. In all the lands from which desirable servants might be drawn—the British Isles, West Germany, the Scandinavian countries—an obvious labor shortage is even now handicapping the industrial programs that are essential to European prosperity. In none of these lands is there the slightest intention of releasing a substantial number of young, active workers. So you may as well mark off immigration as a solution.

Admittedly there is no simple answer—no perfect panacea—to remedy the servant shortage. It now seems probable that we shall presently have, by a process of evolution, a class of skilled homemakers—call them domestic scientists, or what you will. These ably trained domestics will make home management a profession. They may be booked through guilds or agencies in each community, very much as nurses are now assigned, and they will command the prestige and status accorded the registered nurse. The guild will determine the compensation and govern the working conditions. It will also certify the competence and integrity of its members.

If this strikes you as a fanciful forecast you may be surprised to learn that such services now are in operation and are spreading widely. The pattern was set in 1945 by the National Institute of Home Workers, in England, formed for the avowed purpose of "raising the status of domestic work by establishing a skilled craft."

England's domestic ranks were thinned even more drastically than our own during the war years. The distinction is that they began, at an early date, to remedy the situation.

The domestic institute has headquarters in one of the huge country houses on the outskirts of London. There are branches in the principal urban centers of the United Kingdom. It is a government institution, periodically financed by appropriations from Parliament.

In this home atmosphere selected applicants are given an intensive six-month course (nine months for those under seventeen years of age) in modern housekeeping. Instruction is free. Students receive their maintenance and a modest allowance during the training period. A diploma is granted those who pass final examinations. Graduates are entitled to wear the uniform and insignia of the institute. At this point they may enter private service or, at their option, remain with the institute's Daily Home Workers' Service.

In private service the graduate is essentially a free agent, but remains under the general supervision of the institute. The employer must observe certain conditions of the institute code with respect to working conditions and minimum compensation. (These conditions vary in different parts of the country.) The maximum workweek in private service is forty-eight hours, with extra pay for overtime. The employer must grant two weeks' paid vacation annually (three weeks after five years of service).

Graduates of the National Institute of Home Workers are eagerly sought by British households. There are, of course, never a sufficient number to meet the active demand.

In the Daily Home Workers' Service these trained women go into homes on call, ministering to the aged, the ill, and mothers with young children. They are distinctly *housekeepers* and do not duplicate the services of a visiting nurse. Householders pay for these services wholly or in part, according to their respective financial status.

This phase of the institute's program has been widely copied throughout Europe. Norway, which began its "substitute housekeeper" plan in 1947 under the Ministry of Social Affairs, now has service available in more than seven hundred communities. Here, and in the other Scandinavian countries, the "substitute housekeeper" is admittedly an emergency measure. A physician must certify the need. Except by special arrangement, the term of service is limited to three weeks. The applying householder files a certificate of income and pays (if able) a salary that approximates that paid a skilled office worker. In addition the housekeeper (who works an eight-hour day) receives her board and, in some instances, travel compensation.

In the United States emergency housekeeping service is now available in more than a hundred large cities, provided by either a public or a voluntary agency, set up to supervise the program. Though rates vary, housekeepers usually get from $1.50 to $1.75 per hour. As in Europe, most agencies are careful to distinguish between these women and the professional or practical nurse. The housekeeper, for example, is not permitted to administer medicine, although she may remind the patient if the doctor so directs.

Certainly this plan offers no permanent solution of the servant problem, nor is it so intended. It is, as one practitioner observed, "a sort of modern substitute for the maiden aunt who used to make the family rounds 'helping out' in time of need." This program does indicate a trend. From it may in time emerge a broader and more permanent household service.

Some students believe that at least a partial solution may be found in the "housekeeping by contract" idea now under limited test in several communities. With this plan a private company, or perhaps a social agency, would contract to perform specific household services at stipulated intervals for a fixed weekly or monthly fee. The plan has at least the theoretical advantage of relieving a working wife of supervisory responsibilities. The responsibility for rendering competent service is placed upon the contractor. The individual householder evades the Social Security bugaboo and the bother of keeping a record of hours worked. There is, moreover, no concern as to continuity of service. The housewife is assured that the maid will "show up" at an appointed time. It is the contractor's business to see that she, or an acceptable alternate, arrives promptly and labors capably.

Probably we shall never devise an inflexible formula ideally adaptable for all situations. Yet the problem is by no means insoluble. Strange as it may seem to "housework haters," there are women—more of them than you would imagine—who *like* housework; women who have a special, and too often neglected, genius for domestic service. They would prefer to work in a home, under socially acceptable conditions. Our challenge is to get these unattached youngish and middle-aged women into homes where their specialized abilities will be recognized and rewarded; where they may labor with dignity and enduring satisfaction.

XII THE EMERGING ROLE
OF THE SENIOR CITIZEN

TODAY, IN RELATION to the total population there are twice as many persons aged sixty-five or over as there were at the turn of the century. In 1900 the figure was 4.1 per cent of the total population over sixty-five. At present the figure is around 8.1 per cent. The percentage will increase rather steadily during the lifetime of your children and may reach as high as 12 per cent by the time they are ready for retirement.

As we have seen in earlier chapters, a great deal of credit for this increase is due to the fact that we have increased life expectancy in all the age brackets. Naturally this tends to increase the average. Sometimes this is a little difficult for people to understand. Let us try to explain it in this way:

Take a thousand babies born at the turn of the century. From past experience we could calculate that a certain number would thrive, mature and eventually reach the age of sixty-five. We might assume that two hundred of the number would die before celebrating a fifth birthday. Suppose, with improving techniques, we were able to save *half* of those infants. That is a clear gain. Some of those saved are sure to reach the age of sixty-five and thus swell the normal number expected to attain that goal.

Then move on to school age, and we find the process repeated by our virtual banishment of those childhood diseases—typhoid, diphtheria, scarlet fever—that used to keep the little white hearses in such constant use. And how long has it been now since you saw one? If you can keep children out of accidents, they just don't die any more!

And so the story goes at every age bracket. We save a few lives here; a few more there. And some from each bracket live to fatten the "over sixty-five" group. This primarily is the reason for the increase; it is not that people are living so much longer but simply that more of the total number get a fair chance to live out their normal lives.

Nevertheless, we should not underrate the efforts of those who are devoting their specialized talents and time to a study of geriatrics, the special science of the aging. For the first time in history these persons in the sunset years are beginning to get something of a break.

While no one expects in this area the sensational results achieved with, say, infant mortality in the past fifty years, still there is a distinct margin of gain for older individuals in our economy. There has been, for example, continuous improvement in our methods of treating chronic diseases. Earlier diagnosis and treatment offer hope of relief, even if the condition cannot be completely eradicated. New procedures are developed. The use of surgery for older persons is increasing, since they have demonstrated the ability to "take it." Although emphasis is not so much on lowering the death rate in these older persons as it has been on their increased comfort, still the extra years are becoming a definite by-product. Nowadays everyone along the line is getting a better chance to live out his allotted "threescore years and ten." And for a steadily increasing number a healthy bonus looms. *Population Bulletin,* issued by the Population Reference Bureau in Washington, has recently forecast that life expectancy may increase to seventy-five within a generation; indeed it is estimated that white women (who live somewhat longer than men) will have an expectancy above that age by 1970.

Peering a generation into the future we can, of course, only estimate the ratio of persons over sixty-five in relation to the total population. That is because we have no way of estimating birth rates year by year. But it is interesting to note that we can tell almost precisely the gross number of these persons. This is true because the persons who will be sixty-five in another thirty years are now thirty-five years of age. It is merely a case of counting. By the same token we can pretty well determine the size of our work force year by year, twenty years or so in advance. For example, a person born in 1960 will be joining the work force sometime between 1980 and 1985, depending upon the extent of his education.

Adding up the number reaching sixty-five each year and the number joining the work force each year, statisticians are impressed by the fact that for the next twenty years at least we shall be retiring our senior citizens more rapidly than replacements are available. This, at any rate, would be the case if every person reaching sixty-five should retire promptly from the labor market. This, of course, they will not do. Many will continue on the job —some job, somewhere—because they want to work or because they are compelled to do so.

Retirement is a relatively new thing in our social order. In 1890 about 68 per cent of our men over sixty-five kept right on working, chiefly because they couldn't afford to retire. Today only about 39 per cent work beyond sixty-five. And for perhaps a majority of these it is a matter of choice. They work because they would be miserable in idleness.

Compulsory retirement is, and will continue to be, something of a problem to men and women who are ill-prepared for a life of inactivity. Again these senior citizens fall into two groups: those who need more money for fixed expenses than Social

Security will provide and those who are primarily concerned with finding something to occupy their time. Big organizations, generally speaking, will have little place for the over-sixty-five worker. Their hard and fast regulations make it obligatory for him to step down. But there are other organizations glad to have the experience and capabilities of these older people. This will be increasingly the case as our labor market tightens, as it will necessarily do in coming years.

One probable development of the relatively near future would appear to be the thorough revision of Social Security regulations, permitting the individual to draw his monthly check without too rigidly restricting his income from other sources between the years of sixty-five and seventy-two. (Beyond the age of seventy-two a person may now earn whatever he can without in any way affecting Social Security payments.)

This liberalization would doubtless be approved by a majority of our people, including younger workers who now are often obliged to "chip in" and help aged parents or other relatives in retirement. If a man or woman could work and still collect Social Security, obviously more would find some remunerative employment, at least on a part-time basis.

Of course, there is yet another group—those who anticipate retirement with considerable relief and who take to it naturally. They present no special problem since they generally have well-developed plans and always seem to find plenty to occupy their time. "I am so busy these days," declared one recent retiree, "that I often wonder how I ever found the time in the old days to give my business any attention."

Perhaps the greatest single challenge to our social order comes from the executive or upper-level corporation employee who finds himself, perhaps at the very peak of his career, turned out to pasture. He has ample means and he would find it rather humiliating to seek a job in some minor capacity with a smaller firm. A few have found a solution in counseling. But there are definite limits to that field.

Perhaps something approaching a suggestion may be found in the action of two top executives of the East Ohio Gas Company of Cleveland—William C. Rogers, board chairman, and George W. Horsley, senior vice-president. These men are sharing a downtown office in Cleveland, with no telephone and just enough space for both to squeeze in. "It is a place for us to get out of our wives' hair," Rogers explains. "I have had cards printed describing myself as a retired nonconsultant, with no work, no worries, no phone, no prospects, no customers, no nothing."

Although presented in a facetious vein this comment has overtones of tragedy. No one at any point in life should be able to boast of "no worries . . . no prospects . . . no nothing." That is an indication of vegetation. When we cease to grow we begin to grow old.

Some measure of blame must certainly be given the system that, as Dr. Edward L. Bortz, a former president of the American Medical Association, once observed, "with one hand does everything possible to extend the life of man; while with the other, it writes him off as useless because of the date on his birth certificate." At the same time the individual who knows many years in advance what is in store for him cannot be absolved from the responsibility of making some plans for himself. It is incredible that we should spend twenty years in preparation for the forty-year work period, and then give no thought whatsoever to the final years of life which potentially may be the richest and most productive of all. Someone has wisely said that prudent oldsters don't retire; they re-tire for the mileage that still lies ahead of them.

In contrast to the two Cleveland executives consider the case of the board chairman of a large pharmaceutical firm who found himself virtually retired to an advisory post while still full of energy and vigor. Looking around for something to do, this executive very soon found a place for himself with the Chicago Chapter of the American Heart Association. Moving into the downtown office on a volunteer basis he headed a committee to solicit large contributions. Within a week he was compiling lists, writing promotion material, counseling solicitors. What's more important, he was beginning to get results! When I last saw this man he was busier, happier, younger than I had seen him in years.

Note, please, I did not say this executive "looked younger." I said he *was* younger and that is precisely what I meant. The calendar is only one method of measuring age. It can be a most undependable medium. That no two persons are ever the same age, in a realistic sense, is a statement that now has considerable scientific validity. Few of us will argue, I think, that we are not younger at our present age than were our parents at the same calendar stage. People simply do not age as they once did. There are too many stimuli to keep them young. And, of course, as we have observed, people who may have passed the same number of birth anniversaries differ widely in the other age considerations.

It is time we began to give some serious thought to these "young" 65-year-olds in our population. There are plenty of jobs they are ideally fitted to undertake; jobs they could handle with satisfaction to themselves and with profit to the community. Civic organizations, trade associations, luncheon clubs, churches, lodges, public movements of all kinds stand in desperate need of the kind of help the senior citizen is best equipped to give. Some of these, like the job my friend the pharmaceutical board chairman found for himself, may be volunteer occupations. Other undertakings may yield a little remuneration for those who can use a few extra dollars. In any case, the important thing is to find something to do. Something that will take your time and yet enrich your life. The best way to keep young is to feel young. The best way to feel young is to maintain the attitude and viewpoint of the young at heart. Emulate the octogenarian who silenced critics when he showed up at the local blood bank to make a donation. "My blood is as young as anyone's," he insisted. "It just happens to be in an old container."

It may seem premature to make this suggestion. Actually it is not at all out of the way to discuss some phases of eventual retirement with your older children. Agnes E. Meyer, in a very important book on training young people,[1] makes the point that a truly happy old age is not the result of made work or play; it is possible only for individuals who have learned from infancy that by making the most of immediate life they are preparing themselves for a continuously active and productive place in the world.

[1] *Education for a New Morality* (Macmillan).

XIII THE SHIFTING PATTERN
OF POPULATION

PEOPLE DON'T STAY put. That's
one thing you can say for sure. If they did, we'd still be clustered
along the Atlantic seaboard where our forebears settled, reaching
out timidly in each generation to wrest a few more acres from
the wilderness. Almost everything west of the Mississippi River
would still be an Unknown Land.

Fortunately for progress and enterprise, people move. They
get up and get. This makes for interesting speculation on the
movement of populations. But actually here in the United States
there is not a great deal of occasion for speculation. We have
seen these movements so clearly marked in recent years that
almost everyone accepts the fact that certain areas will advance
more rapidly than others. The South, the Southwest and the
Pacific Coast are notable examples. Our primary questions involve the rate and rapidity of expansion.

We have now almost taken for granted that Florida and California will pace each other for the settlement of our senior
citizens when they reach retirement age. Florida has some advantages geographically. People of the congested Northland can more
readily get down to look it over. Having spent several pleasant

vacations there, they are more susceptible to its lures as a permanent residence. It has, of course, the advantage of more water, not only the ocean and the gulf, but myriad lakes of varying size as well.

On the other hand, California is considered by many a more suitable climate, particularly for those afflicted with arthritic or kindred ills.

And there's always the Southwest—Arizona, New Mexico and the adjacent states, all with powerful appeal for those who have once looked upon their beauty.

So, at the head of our little list of reasons for population shifts let us write "climate" with the primary thought of elderly persons seeking pleasant surroundings for retirement.

This is a relatively new idea in our world. When I was a boy very few persons ever sought a change of climate unless they chanced to be sufferers from tuberculosis and went by doctor's orders on a journey of desperation. The general run of ordinary people born in a community expected to live their lives there unless some fortuitous chance of trade took them to a neighboring town or perhaps even to another state. True, some of the restless young ones moved away. Once you got past forty, however, you settled down. The home town was your town. You expected to live there the rest of your days and be buried from the white meetinghouse on the hill.

That is no longer true. Nowadays almost everyone you talk to has plans. They hope to "get away from these winters"; to "go to some warm climate and retire." My reference is not exclusively, or even primarily, to persons of means. Have a talk with your postman. Or the man who delivers your milk. At least one will have his ideas pretty well pat. His eyes will sparkle as he tells you how he has it figured out.

I admit to considerable apprehension over this trend. People who have established friendships in a community, who have played cards with the same groups for thirty years, are not easily uprooted. I fear they may be in for disappointment and disillusion, at a time of life when naturally they may be subject to the depressions of age. I have seen too many of these lonely old people "sitting it out in the sun" to dismiss the prospect lightly.

There is a vast difference between going away for a few weeks in the winter and pulling up stakes permanently. A vacation in Florida or California? By all means, if you can manage it. But think long and carefully before you retire to any place except your own familiar community.

There isn't a great deal we can do about this trend right now beyond issuing our counsel to any who care to listen. But we can prognosticate.

I believe with considerable conviction that by the time your children reach mature years this most unwise urge to make retirement a distinct and radical break in the life pattern shall have spent its course and that we may anticipate a healthier attitude toward our sunset years.

Probably ahead of climate in the number of persons affected, and certainly in the total of disruptions, we have our commercial changes. More and more these days the big companies—and many smaller ones—have their scattered factories and branch offices. For some reason they must keep up a febrile shuffling of "the organization." Every shuffle means a move for somebody's family. We speak of this as "putting out new roots." It is more accurately a case of trying to cover all old roots with enough soil to give some deceptive semblance of permanency.

A young matron whose husband is in the Public Health Service (two-year moves) recently bespoke her teen-age daughter's apprehension. "Margie is so afraid Dave's transfer will come through before she can graduate with her high school group. She has been with the class for a year and a half now, and feels so attached to the group."

Certainly this is an age of mobility. The ease and speed of modern transportation invites us to hustle and bustle from hither to yon. There is still something to be said for serenity. Surely the young householder has a right to a few years of "settled-downness" while his family is in the process of growing up. This is an important right for your children, and for their children as well. Give it a passing thought.

The moves that have directly to do with industry are the more impelling because they often have to do directly with bread and butter, or the prospective lack of it. People have been leaking out of New England slowly for generations because it is a hard, bitter country that gives grudgingly to those who invest in it their talents and their toil. New England agriculture has been petering out. Yields cannot compare with the bounties of generous Midwestern acres. More recently New England has been losing her traditional industries, losing them chiefly to the Southeast, where an intelligent, sturdy mountain labor still may be had in abundance. Textile mills in particular have been hard hit. Workers are widely scattered. Factories can operate more economically from the edge of a cotton field or near the resources for synthetic fabrics.

Conditions of this sort have ever prevailed in industrial lands. They make for a pattern of slow but inevitable change. We grieve for the old buggy-whip factory out on the edge of town that in its heyday met the grocery bills of fifty families. We hated to see it go. After all, if no one buys whips, even the most stubborn and perverse entrepreneurs can't be expected to continue using up resources and capital to pile up a useless inventory. Come to think of it, the site of that old whip plant is now the location of a bustling little plant making television antennas. Weren't we reading just the other day that they now employ more than five hundred persons? This offsets the whip-factory loss tenfold, but of course in the transition period a lot of good whip men had to leave town looking for some kind of jobs to feed their families.

It is this sort of thing that is going on all the time in America—the restless jostling for jobs. That the smarter boys tend to leave our small towns is an accepted commonplace. Whether the opportunities always are greater in the big cities may be a question. Youth believes that they are, and the net effect is motion. The quest for opportunity has indeed always been a potent factor in altering our population pattern. It sent the pioneers plunging westward, first to the Mississippi and then on to the Pacific Coast. Yes, sometimes in quest of gold or other treasure, but often seeking nothing beyond the prosaic pattern of a few fertile acres with plenty of room to stretch. It is this same yearning for substance and status that sends our Southern Negroes northward and leads the marginal unfortunates in our great cities to try their fortunes in booming Alaska or Hawaii.

There are other phases of population movement that more directly concern us. They may have greater relevancy to the future of your children.

We may concern ourselves briefly with the movement from our cities to the suburbs. There is too much visual evidence of this movement for anyone to doubt its validity. At the last accounting our suburbs were growing seven times more rapidly than the central cities. One cannot scoff at such statistics.

Five years ago I would have given odds that your children would settle in the suburbs. Possibly in a place somewhat like the one you now occupy "only farther out." I am now not quite so sure.

I must admit there is very little supporting evidence as these lines are written, but a simple underlying truth is that Suburbia is going sour.

Please don't misunderstand me. The suburbs will continue to grow. There will be finer houses and more of them. More and more people moving in all the time. It's a trend. And you don't stop a trend in it's tracks.

Those portions of Suburbia peopled by a generation that grew up in small towns or on a farm probably are on pretty solid ground. You can take that literally. They have an understanding of the soil; an affection for it. But there are too many people cluttering up the suburbs today who have only an urban culture, an urban point of view. They belong in the cities. The sooner they get back to them the better for all concerned.

Some of these people who, for their own good, should be shooed from Suburbia have considerable money. Others are flailing debts with both hands. The latter group, up from the tenements, the rooming houses, the unfashionable back streets, are the ones who bought those flimsy, shoe-box houses in those fabulous close-in developments. Row after row of unimaginative block houses, each with its blotting-pad patch of lawn.

"When I have to be at home," says a young serviceman, one of many thousands saddled with such disillusioning properties, "I spend half my time spitting from my window into the bedroom of my neighbor on the east. The rest of the time I spend answering the telephone of my neighbor on the west, in the belief that it's my ring."

And the people with money? They are the ones responsible for the huge market centers, the slick city shops, the ten-story co-operative apartments, all set down in what used to be pleasant little country places in which to live. This invasion is forcing the real lovers of the suburbs to retreat farther and farther along side roads and bypaths. Even this has its dangers. You are either running into the edges of another city or else someone is likely to launch a sixty-acre subdivision all around you. This, incidentally, is the true suburbanite's picture of Hell Incarnate. To prevent such a catastrophe he is likely to load himself down with more property than he possibly can care for. Finally, when he's feeling a little secure, a neighbor to the north sells ten acres for a real estate development. Soon all the new householders are tootling down our friend's little lane, which turns out to be the only outlet to a paved road.

It is perhaps stretching reality a bit to suggest that there are persons born with "city" genes, just as there are others born with genes that impel them toward life in the country. If this is putting the situation a bit too fatalistically, there are, we must at least concede, definite "city" types. These are for the most part people born in the city or brought to it in early life. They thrive on the hustle and bustle, the throngs and bongs. The constant drone of traffic, with its not infrequent overtones of thunder, is a melody. Theirs is a flex-muscled music and they will have no part of pastoral simplicity. They may reside in the sybaritic splendor of a penthouse or represent the washed-up scum of the slums. In either case, they belong in the city, and though it may take a few years for the disillusioning fact to sink in, these people are miserable away from the downtown district. They ought to get back.

One of the problems is that we haven't any suitable place to put them. For more than a decade construction has been centered on Suburbia. We have built houses on the edge of town and moved people out to them in wholesale lots. Meanwhile, their former homes in the city have been demolished to make parking lots or have deteriorated beyond hope of habitation.

One of the primary problems confronting your children will be that of rebuilding our central cities. It is a problem that cannot be too long delayed, because the central city is the heart of the whole metropolitan tax structure. We cannot permit it to die—and many of our downtown districts are rapidly deteriorating—else we risk a collapse of catastrophic proportions.

Almost everyone agrees that America's metropolitan areas suffer from "downtown decay." Two contributing factors are absentee ownership (the chain-store operating system) and the fact that most downtown land is now under 99-year leases (which means that landlords have no direct responsibility for the structures and are interested solely in collecting rents).

The centers of our great cities are at least a quarter of a

century behind the calendar. We can ill afford that, because our great urban centers represent 60 per cent of the nation's invested wealth. These investments are withering at so rapid a rate that specialists have raised the fear that urban investments may be ruined in the active lifetime of your children.

Landlords generally have neither the means nor the incentive to modernize. However, there are human values involved which the community as a whole cannot afford to ignore. As one observer has pointed out, "If the central city collapses, the outer suburbs will have lost their way of life." Many of the chronic problems, such as traffic congestion and the clearance of blighted areas, are matters for co-operative action.

Unless citizens consent to remake their present tax pattern, allocating more personal income to local taxes for personal services (and this is the only realistic solution), some government aid will be required along the way.

Federal aid to our cities is going to become a very real issue. Action cannot be too long postponed. After all, it is a matter that vitally concerns eight times as many persons as now live on all our farms. (And just look what we've spent on the "farm problem!")

Today more than two thirds of the total American population live in metropolitan areas. True, a steadily growing proportion of these are suburban dwellers. But they are none the less interested in a healthy downtown district. In a great many instances their payroll checks come from there! When an urban community suffers from heart trouble the entire corporate structure is impaired.

Dr. Luther Gulick, director of the New York Bureau of Municipal Research, has gone so far as to term metropolitan reconstruction the foundation of our national power. He sees it as a necessary and inescapable responsibility of the federal government where cities fail to meet the challenge.

Senator Joseph S. Clark, Jr., of Pennsylvania, the one-time

Democratic mayor of Philadelphia, who knows the problem intimately, has been periodically introducing bills in Congress urging
a Cabinet post to handle urban affairs. Early action on Senator
Clark's measure is hardly to be expected. Some educational effort
will be necessary. At any rate, the problem is beginning to
receive attention.

As we have already intimated, a considerable number of those
families who made quick, emotionally inspired treks to the
country are beginning to get what might be termed "a bellyful
of the bucolic." Their thoughts turn wistfully toward town. A
considerable number of them are going to have to move as their
shabby, close-in, claptrap houses become virtually uninhabitable
long before the twenty-year mortgages are paid out. The question
of where to put the returning pilgrims is a persistent problem.
In our concentration on developing the suburbs no one has given
much thought to central city housing.

Talking to a convention of the National Association of Real
Estate Boards some months ago, Dr. George Cline Smith, a vice-
president of the F. W. Dodge Corporation, foremost statisticians
of the building industry, pointed out that at our present construction rate it would take 181 years just to replace our present stock
of city housing. This is approximately the length of time the United
States has been in existence. Obviously houses in this twentieth
century were never constructed for any such period of servitude.
The simple fact of the matter, therefore, is that we are not
replacing our older houses.

In some instances, to be sure, the growing needs of mercantile
establishments are usurping areas once devoted to residences.
That is to be expected in any large city. But in virtually every
urban center, and even in many county-seat towns, once-desirable
residential areas are withering, primarily because older houses
have not been replaced or modernized.

Most of us have had the experience of being driven around a

strange city. Motoring past rows of drab structures, obviously of the Teddy-and-Taft era—many of them now converted into rooming houses—our host may say apologetically, "Just a few years ago this was one of our better residential areas."

What has happened? Why have whole sections of our modern cities fallen to such low estate? What can be done about it? The problem is a serious one not only for the individual property owner but for the municipality as well. Centrally located real estate that should be steadily accelerating in value is bringing in less and less income from taxes.

It may be argued that with the strong suburban trend there is sluggish demand for houses in town. If that be true it is chiefly because available town houses are obsolete, dilapidated, and generally undesirable. An appealing, centrally located house of contemporary design will find a buyer at a good price. This will be increasingly true in the next ten or fifteen years as more of the disillusioned turn back to town.

In my judgment the next residential renaissance will be in our central cities. Already several municipalities are experimenting with attractive new types of group residential construction. We shall see more and more of these developments sponsored both by city fathers and by farseeing private investors. Perhaps some of the better-constructed co-operative apartments which we mentioned as a threat to the suburbs may find a welcome haven in our central cities.

One should not infer from all this that suburban life in America is endangered, that it is likely to wither and deteriorate. Quite the contrary. Suburban existence is a firmly fixed pattern in our modern lives. The suburbs will continue to flourish and prosper.

Whether your children will live in the suburbs depends upon a number of factors, including background, inclinations, family status, nature of occupation, and so on. In the upper middle class chances are a little better than even that they will become suburban dwellers. If they have come from a small town or suburban background, chances are considerably enhanced. With small children the suburbs obviously have their complications. They also have compensations that tend to outweigh the difficulties.

In the lifetime of your children we may expect to see our moderate-sized cities extended to a point where the suburbs will reach to the nearest county-seat town in practically any direction. (Even now, of course, the suburban areas of our large cities extend much farther than that.) The time may not be too distant when a householder out to take his family for a Sunday ride may have to drive fifty miles or more to see a cornfield or a cow.

One of the newer developments attracting considerable attention these days is the "strip city." Some authorities have suggested that within twenty years the United States will be dominated by about fifteen of these metropolitan strips. They point to the first of these, now virtually complete—the strip extending from Maine to Virginia along the East Coast. Once a series of independent markets, this strip now is virtually one single city some six hundred miles in length. It contains less than 2 per cent of the country's land area but represents more than a fifth of the population and nearly one fourth of all retail sales.

These strips—they are called "interurbias"—form continuous concentrated areas of industrial development, with suburban areas extending into the hinterlands on either side. Often it is difficult to tell when you are passing from one city into another. Strips similar to the East Coast development are springing up all over the country. One of the notable ones now rapidly taking shape is the Lake Michigan area. It begins roughly at South Bend, Indiana, extending through Gary and Hammond to Chicago and northward through Waukegan to Kenosha, Racine and Milwaukee.

XIV TOMORROW'S MANNERS, MODES AND MORES

OUR DAILY LIVES are considerably influenced by fashions, fads and foibles. To an even greater extent we are motivated by long-range trends, such as the strong trend toward smaller families which has been discussed in earlier chapters. Fashion may determine the cut of your next season's apparel, but trends shape the course of your life for a generation.

Between these two forces, and in a sense more impelling than either, are our collective life habits. They often are extremely helpful to the analyst in determining the shape of future life patterns. In this effort to peer into the future there is no element of necromancy or fortunetelling. It is purely a matter of deduction. It is impossible to anticipate the specific reactions of any one individual. However, we can tell with considerable accuracy the probable course of a collective group some twenty-five or fifty years hence.

For example, let us turn to the matter of cigarette smoking. I can see no marked change in the smoking habits of your teen-aged children. They are pretty well conditioned by example and custom. A considerable number of them will smoke cigarettes. Your children of preschool age will be a little less likely to smoke.

I predict that by the turn of the century the cigarette smoker in our social order will be as conspicuous as the nonsmoker now is.

I make this forecast not primarily from visible signs—although there are portents for those who seek them—but from the fact that cigarette smoking is a habit, and habits change. They operate on what I term the "accordion principle"—just so much expansion and then the contraction sets in.

If my suggestion of a radical change in cigarette smoking seems preposterous, I invite your attention to the fact that a century ago every gentleman of quality dipped snuff. (Desks in the cloakrooms of House and Senate in Washington still are equipped with ornate snuffboxes and these are kept filled with fresh snuff, although probably no member of either house now uses tobacco in that form.)

The cigarette-smoking habit is about due for a change. It has passed the daring or exciting stage. There is no longer any lure or distinction in smoking cigarettes. It is a habit the bank president shares with the street cleaner. And both of them at times wish they didn't have it.

Cigarettes started toward their culminating production peak about thirty-five years ago when they began making tentative bids for the feminine contingent. Middle-aged people still recall when the woman smoker was a rarity and almost never encountered in public. (At a somewhat earlier period Teddy Roosevelt's daughter shocked Washington society with her cigarette puffing in hotels and clubs.)

It must have been about 1925 that the makers of Chesterfield cigarettes took the tentative step, picturing a young couple seated on a grassy knoll. The man was contentedly smoking a Chesterfield. The caption "Blow some my way!" was the first bold suggestion that a female could possibly tolerate tobacco smoke. Within two or three years women were being pictured in the ads smoking in their own right. Now, of course, their appearances outnumber the men.

No one can ever know the number of young men who took up cigarette smoking as a symbol of maturity; because it was the smart, masculine thing to do. That compulsion is rapidly disappearing. Smoking is now so commonly accepted as to arouse no particular feeling one way or another. This is one of the indications that a change is brewing in our social attitude toward cigarettes. In Europe, where cigarettes are much more expensive than here, the tendency away from smoking, especially in the younger generation, is clearly marked. Groups are being formed to pledge abstinence and to aid each other in breaking the habit. Two years ago I had occasion to discuss this matter with a number of European educators. They all agreed that the movement is very real and producing tangible results. As the headmistress of an English school for girls summed up the situation: "It simply is no longer considered smart to smoke."

If you look for visual evidence of a slowdown in cigarette smoking, I admit there is not a great deal to go on. We all know individuals who, influenced by scare headlines or other considerations, have stopped smoking. This doesn't appear to have had much effect on cigarette consumption. Each year the makers record a new high in sales volume. However, a closer study reveals a faint but discernible pattern of deterioration.

For one thing, we must recall that cigarette sales are commonly reported in the newspapers in dollars. The switch to filter tips has resulted in an increase of 15 to 25 per cent in cost without increasing tobacco consumption. Moreover, these sales quoted in retail volume may include steadily increasing state and federal taxes.

Then, too, there is the consideration that confirmed smokers tend to increase their consumption of tobacco. The man who smoked a pack a day ten years ago may now find himself edging up to around a pack and a half or two packs. This tends normally to boost consumption without increasing the number of addicts.

However, unless there is a constant stream of new smokers, the old ones die off and their volume cannot be replaced.

So far the stream has continued. It will continue for a few more years perhaps. The significant point is that in the past five years American cigarette producers, excluding imports, have done little better than hold their own. They have not kept pace with increasing population. And that is a very revealing sign.

So I say, with considerable conviction, that *cigarette* smoking over a period of fifty years will decline materially. Please note the emphasis on that term "cigarette." I pointedly do not say that Americans will not step up their consumption of cigars and pipe tobacco. Nor do I hold it beyond the limits of possibility that some completely new form of tobacco ingestion may be invented. And of course there is always the possibility that cigarette smoking may be superseded by some even more objectionable habit. You recall the old gag concerning Tobacco Anonymous: When you feel the urge for a cigarette, call a specified number. They will send over two guys to get drunk with you!

Habits are, of course, not the only factor shaping our lives. Circumstances often dictate courses of action which become rather firmly fixed.

Forty years ago no woman deemed in her right mind would have dreamed of driving an automobile. That was man's work and, moreover, a task reserved for the hardier and more adventurous males.

Now we approach a point where it is safe to say that women will become our primary drivers of motor vehicles. Even now in many households—perhaps a clear majority—the wife does more driving than the husband. In suburban homes she not only motors him to the railway station but also uses the family car for marketing and assorted errands and, in addition, chauffeurs the children to their varied social engagements.

Already this role is taken as a matter of course. Give the

suburban wife-mother another twenty-five years and she will automatically take her place at the steering wheel when the family is off for an outing. Father will gratefully relax with his cigar. Driving is woman's work!

Now let us devote a few words to the subject of manners. Some will readily assert that a few words should suffice since manners are admittedly in short supply. This is especially true in matters relating to our reverence for the female species. This growing disregard of little attentions to our womenfolk is a long-range trend; a consequence of woman's growing independence and aggressiveness. As woman has demonstrated a desire and an ability to look after herself, man has been less disposed to extend his protective arm.

Curiously enough, this whole business of reverencing womankind en masse is an American notion. The gentlemen who originated the reverence-for-women routine back in the days when knighthood was in flower would have been pretty much appalled at the idea of extending the deferential routine to all forms of femininity. They pedestaled certain highborn women and these alone were to be reverenced and extended special courtesies and considerations. The general run of women were, to the average knight, slightly inferior to the general run of men, which was equivalent to giving them a pretty low rating indeed.

This concept of the pedestaled woman was about as ridiculous as the idea of knighthood itself. But it proved a great deal more enduring. Throughout most of Europe the highborn women—the patricians—were accorded special courtesies and considerations by their men. (Naturally both sexes were revered by the more lowly classes.) It was these European aristocrats who fostered the creed that women of their class were entitled to rather special consideration solely on the ground that they were born into the world in female form and fashion. Naturally the women—patrician women—did nothing to dispel this theory. On the contrary, they were at some pains to inculcate the idea firmly in the minds of their young males. So the tradition carried on.

In due course some of these patricians emigrated to America and established plantations in the Southland. Since, in most areas, they represented the only white women in the community, the idea naturally became established that deference was to be paid to all (white) womankind on the basis of sex rather than patrician antecedents. In the fullness of several generations the young Southern lad came to a point where he tipped his cap not only to his schoolteacher but also to the cleaning woman, the seamstress, and presumably even the town harlot if he chanced to encounter her journeying from her cloistered domicile.

It was these migrating Southern boys, and an aristocratic fringe from New England, who brought "manners" to America. In no other land has there ever been comparable regard for the female without regard to individual status.

Now these manners are dying out. We may regret the passage but we may as well reconcile ourselves to the obvious facts of modern life. Already there are abundant evidences of deterioration from turn-of-the-century standards. It doesn't take much imagination to surmise what is ahead.

Twenty years from now, in all probability, little Ewald will not tip his hat to the ladies he meets. As a matter of fact, the chances are better than even that his father doesn't do so now. Let two good friends of assorted sexes meet by chance on the street. If the man is wearing a hat he will often keep it on while greeting the lady with genuine enthusiasm.

Women have battled for and achieved equality in business and related circles. And men apparently feel that this fact precludes preferment in the social niceties. If an executive and his guests arose every time a secretary came into the office on an errand they would resemble jumping jacks.

The same practical motives perhaps have led men to abandon

the practice of removing hats in crowded office elevators. Hats in hand take up added space. For some reason they still take off hats quite generally in hotel elevators. Most of the time men will crowd to either side of an open elevator while women in the rear elbow their way to the exit. Even these symbols of polite society will pass with time. Give them another twenty years.

It is a little sad to contemplate the passing of so pleasant an era. It was very nice while it lasted.

Particularly for women.

XV

THE RISING TIDE
OF TOLERANCE:

Our New Morality

AL SMITH ONCE attended a political conference in an Eastern city which broke up at two o'clock on a Sunday morning. At five o'clock Al was routed out of his warm hotel bed to attend an early morning Mass.

In the grim dawn of a winter morning Smith looked up at the darkened windows where his Protestant friends were still peacefully snoring. His teeth chattering, he turned to two companions and remarked, "Just suppose it should turn out that they were right after all!"

This anecdote is illustrative of a feeling that is springing up all over America these days. A feeling that may be defined as the Rising Tide of Tolerance. This is especially true if we may define tolerance in some youngster's comment that it is the sneaking suspicion the other side may have inside information. Never has the average man been so free to doubt his own convictions, so ready to accommodate himself to the other fellow's point of view.

Nor is tolerance limited to religious issues. It extends quite literally to every avenue of life. Nor do we have to seek for an answer to our question of why tolerance has suddenly become ascendant. Since intolerance is to a considerable degree the product of ignorance and stupidity, it is only reasonable to assume that as our avenues of communication are opened, as we become better informed on a variety of issues, tolerance should become more marked in our midst. As we open minds we automatically close doors to torrents of prejudice and suspicion. And these are the prime raw materials of which intolerance is fabricated.

Tolerance is the only real test of civilization. We still have far too many festering pockets of ignorance and prejudice for us to view the scene with any great degree of satisfaction. Although we tend to associate intolerance with the lower economic groups, it is by no means their exclusive property. The germs do their damage indiscriminately to all types of human beings and they are, as someone has observed, as indiscriminate as chicken pox, while having a mortality rate more closely resembling cancer or tuberculosis.

How much tolerance we have in the world twenty-five years hence may very well depend on the lessons you are teaching your children today. To teach your child the principles of tolerance in his relations with his fellows is to place in his hands the tools for marked preferment and rapid advancement.

If what I said at the outset may have given you the impression that religious intolerance is a thing of the past, certainly there is sufficient evidence about us to refute that opinion. True, the average man is adjusting himself to religious differences with his neighbor. When that neighbor's spiritual rights are impinged or his temple is defiled, we fight for him with vigor and vehemence. But there still are bigots battling on sectarian fronts, and there probably will continue to be so long as the "Big Three" remain relatively powerful. We can all manage to be sympathetic with the little fellow, even though we disagree with his philosophy. However, to tolerate strengths equal to or even surpassing our own—that takes character and vision.

Let us return to our average citizen and his religious accommodation. "Tolerance," said Joshua Loth Liebman, "is the positive and cordial effort to understand another's beliefs, practices and habits without necessarily sharing or accepting them." In this one area of life modern man in America has come very close to abdicating his own beliefs in a frenzied effort to accommodate himself to the philosophies of others. Our reference is, of course, to the religious life. However, we must candidly consider whether this is so much a matter of furthering neighborly relations as it is a condition of personal indifference. In any case, the typical American, be he Protestant, Catholic or Hebrew, no longer leads a meaningful affirmative life in any realistic religious sense. He exists, rather, by a series of social concepts carefully adjusted to the one significant objective of getting along with the other fellow.

Oh, to be sure, our typical American stands up in his house of worship on the Sabbath and mouths a collection of ritualistic words that, for him, have long since lost any semblance of personal meaning. Grandfather's ringing affirmation has given way to a new order of word construction expressing the tide of tolerance.

"I believe . . . !" is now supplanted by, "Brother, you may be right!"

What does this average man actually believe, in a religious sense?

To be entirely candid in the matter, he himself would have considerable trouble giving a satisfactory answer. Thoughts on religion bring up so many imponderables that he infinitely prefers to tuck the whole matter away into an inner recess of his mind and refer to it as infrequently as possible.

He does believe in some sort of a Supreme Being. He has no very clear notion of what this God is like. But he feels instinctively that God must exist, because such an assumption is more reasonable than to conclude that the whole universe was self-created from hopeless chaos.

To an orderly mind that line of thought is incomprehensible. So, yes, there must be a God. That God must have created man, along with everything else on the earth. That being so, he must have some sort of plan for his creatures. He must exercise some manner of guidance over their destiny. Thus a plea to the Creator when you really are in trouble makes sense. It can't do any harm. And it just might help.

On the question of eternal life the average man believes superficially, chiefly because his early religious training precludes flat negation. He doesn't dast to say no. Besides, what harm is there to believe? He has nothing to lose. Unlike earlier generations in a harder world, modern man doesn't spend much time thinking about heaven. He is pretty well satisfied with his present spot here on earth and is in no hurry to move along. To an individual who sometimes finds it difficult to find satisfying employment for a rainy Sunday afternoon, the prospect of an eternity of blissful idleness is not particularly intriguing.

To sum up, our average man *hopes* there is a life beyond the grave. If so, he feels that he has a rather good chance of participating in it. But the entire matter absorbs precious little of his thought. His convictions in the matter probably are less firmly fixed than his opinions on the population of neighboring planets.

The Bible? He respects and reverences it as a holy document. He believes the Old Testament was wrought slowly and painfully by inspired men who were very close to the Creator. That it was related to a simple people in the myths and legends of the time seems to him a perfectly natural development. In this spirit he accepts Noah in the ark and Daniel in the den. They are symbols and their precise authenticity is a matter of no particular concern.

If our average man is a Protestant he hardly knows what to believe with respect to the New Testament. The exploitation of the Deep Sea Scrolls and other developments of our decade have left him badly shaken. In another ten or fifteen years, when these discoveries have been more completely assimilated and evaluated, he will be on firmer ground. For the moment he is rather disposed to accept the New Testament story because he has no firm alternative. Oh, yes—yes, he believes in the divinity of Jesus Christ. But don't push him too closely on that issue of the Immaculate Conception.

So, again we say it comes down pretty much to this: Our man doesn't quite know what he thinks and would just as soon not give the matter too much scrutiny. For himself he has worked out a sort of pattern of ethical conduct to which he tries right manfully to adhere. On the whole he does pretty well. Vaguely he thinks of himself as a religious man. He believes in the church. More of his number are currently church-affiliated than at any other period in our national history. Our man supports the church more bountifully than his occasional presence in a pew would indicate. He wants his children to attend Sunday school and to be "brought up" within the folds of the church. Beyond this point he doesn't do much worrying.

Looking at this outline of our religious convictions and the behavior pattern of the average man, at this point a little beyond the middle of the twentieth century, the sociologist can reach only one conclusion: A gradual amalgamation of Judaistic-Christian social concepts will eventually result in something very like a common working religion. The churches, the temples, the synagogues will stand for a very long time. Because these symbols are rooted in the traditions of the centuries and their votaries are uncommonly adhesive. Outside and beyond these symbols the people—as they have before in human history—will be seeking their destiny elsewhere. Penitent and chastened they may return to their divisional houses of worship—as they have done before. That only time can tell.

Your children will continue to see the people of our land abandoning their traditions to clamber aboard the ark of the One Great God as it rides high the rising tide of tolerance.

XVI THE DECLINE AND DOOM OF TEDIOUS TOIL

WHEN A MATRON of my acquaintance was five years of age she was taken by her grandmother to visit a nearby city. There, for the first time, she beheld sweating, dirt-streaked men engaged in digging a ditch. She was deeply disturbed that such things had to be and questioned her grandmother at length as to why such a state of affairs should be permitted.

Grandmother was equal to the occasion. "Now, darling," she said soothingly, "you are not to trouble your head for a moment about such matters. There have always been two kinds of people in the world. There must always continue to be. There are the plebeians to hew the wood and draw the water; and there are the patricians who live in comfort from the labors of the more lowly. That is the way the world is made up. There is nothing you or I can do about it. Now, you finish your ice-cream soda or we'll be late for the picture show."

Grandmother was a patrician.

Undoubtedly the indifference of patricians to the fate of the lowly has slowed by decades a more equitable distribution of labor. Even now it is not the compassion for plebeians but the

146

growing cheapness of electricity and other energy sources that has emancipated the laboring throng. Kilowatts have become cheaper than muscles. At the same time there has been a steadily increasing demand for people with a little more "book learning" and background to operate all this new machinery. The consequence has been, as I have observed in earlier chapters, that we are educating our people out of drudgery and into a higher type of service for the community. The result will be the decline and eventual doom of tedious toil.

We are not at that point yet nor shall we be within the lifetime of your children. Unquestionably, there is a great deal less tedious toil in the country than there was a decade ago. There will be even less a decade hence. There will be some, however. There will be tasks that are dreary and dull and highly unpleasant. And someone will have to do them.

There will be people ready. Strange as it may seem to the effete, there are persons who prefer to exercise brawn over brain. They don't want thinking jobs. They want to be garbage collectors because there's good money in it. Yes, that is the catch. Once we paid a very low rate for our menial tasks because there were a great many people available who could do nothing else. They had to take what we offered or starve. No more. Brawn workers are in short supply. They have to be paid on a par with the brain workers or they'll take the next handy job. Of course even the "brawns" are smarter than they once were. They have to be. Because even they must handle complicated machinery and keep simple records. In another twenty years you will hardly find a man anywhere who doesn't have—and have use for—a grammar school education.

It should not be assumed that, because we are in some degree putting drudgery on the shelf, your children will of necessity settle down happily to such labors as come their way. There has been a great deal of rank foolishness written concerning the Joy of the Job. This may be as good a place as any to dissipate some of it.

In the United States today there are more than 65 million persons gainfully employed. Some recent statistics indicate that about half of these men and women experience no great sense of satisfaction from their daily labors. There are prophets who forecast that this percentage is likely to increase.

Isn't it, therefore, about time to discard some of our more persistent notions concerning the Glory of Labor and the moral compulsion to glean joy from the job?

When our nation was young and primitive, dreary drudgery and ceaseless toil were the common lot of man. There was no acceptable alternative. So our early forebears invented the myth that labor is ennobling; preached a philosophy of salvation-through-sweat. In those days the honest husbandman who found no delight in diligence faced scant recompense indeed, save in the hope of heaven.

So the myth was a societal necessity. But it was a pure invention. There is no foundation for it in any enduring moral code. You will search Holy Writ in vain for a testimonial to the Joy of the Job. On the contrary, the curse of the Creator upon Adam is revealed by the decree: "In the sweat of thy face shalt thou eat bread."

"To business that we love," said Shakespeare, "we rise betime and go to 't with delight." But all over this land, it must be said, multiplied millions rise reluctantly and go to their labors with resignation rather than rejoicing.

This is a great pity. An even graver tragedy lies in the fact that these unhappy workers carry with them an added burden— a conviction of guilt engendered by a shabby, threadbare Puritan precept. They feel, vaguely and uneasily, a sense of failure. There *should* be pleasure in work—and it isn't there. This frustration is a fare to nourish neuroses.

We all have to work. But we don't have to *like* it. That is
a simple truth that badly needs reiteration. To face with indifference, or even active distaste, tasks that seem to us menial or
meaningless is a perfectly natural reaction. There is in this attitude
nothing either abnormal or immoral. Certainly there are a
favored and fortunate few who find in their occupations full
opportunity for the release of energies and enthusiasms. There
may be soul satisfaction in designing a fleet new motorcar.
However, there is precious little stimulation in endlessly tightening
nut A–16 on an assembly line. It is pretty unrealistic to pretend
that there is.

So what, then, is our counsel to our children who may find
their work a chore or a bore?

First, if you are numbered among the dissident workers,
analyze your individual situation. Do you have precisely in mind
a type of congenial employment for which you have special aptitude and training? Exclude those nebulous dreams of "a better
job." For we are concerned now only with well-defined desires.
If you have unusual qualifications for another type of work—
something you believe sincerely will prove more congenial—and
if you are in a position to make the move—then take steps to get
the work you want. You may not be any happier in the new
vocation—there is drudgery and frustration in every occupation.
But you have every right to try.

Let us assume, however, that you are compelled by necessity,
or impelled by prudence, to remain in your present position.
Having come to this reasoned conclusion, accept the situation
philosophically. You still have a precious gift—a gift no earlier
generation could claim in such abundant measure. You have
time—time of your own, to spend as you will.

This gift of time is a relatively new grant in our workaday
world. As recently as 1870 one of Chicago's leading department
stores opened its doors daily at 7 A.M., closed at 8 P.M., except

Saturday, when the closing hour was 9 P.M. Clerks were expected
to be on hand well before the opening hour and to put their
stocks in order after the store closed for the day. They were
required to sweep floors; dust furniture, shelves and showcases;
trim wicks, fill lamps, clean chimneys—and even make their own
quill pens! In addition, a store bulletin of the period decreed
that each male clerk "shall bring in a bucket of water and a
scuttle of coal for the day's business."

It is to be assumed that an average employee hadn't much
energy for mischief after a fourteen-hour day on such a job. Still
a benevolent employer took no chances:

> Each employee will attend fast meeting on Thursday. Also
> you are expected to attend your Sunday school.
>
> Any employee who smokes Spanish cigars, uses liquor in
> any form, gets shaved at the barber shop, frequents pool
> halls or public dance halls, will give his employer every
> reason to suspicion his integrity, worthy intentions and all-
> around honesty.

And this was counted one of the more enlightened and progressive establishments of the late nineteenth century!

Well, we have journeyed quite a distance sociologically in
ninety years. Now, with the changing scene, you have many more
hours to devote to activities beyond your daily occupation. Have
you ever considered how much time you really have? Let's see:

Twenty-four hours a day multiplied by seven yields a total
of 168 hours a week. That's all the time there is. No one anywhere can possibly manage a minute more. To an average job,
these days, you probably devote no more than 40 hours a week.
This leaves a balance of 128 hours—more than three quarters of
your total time. This is theoretically "free" time, to invest as you
will. Of course, you must eat and sleep. So let's make another
deduction of 12 hours a day—84 hours a week—half of your
original allotment. And what have we left? There is a balance

of 44 hours of leisure—*actually, more than the total time you devote to your daily job!* And we haven't even taken into account your holidays and paid vacation!

With these precious hours firmly in your grasp you may now turn to any avocation your heart desires. Run down the alphabet of hobbies and make your choice—anything from tinkering with automobiles to playing the zither. Surely lack of time is no longer a valid excuse for inaction. We need only a commanding interest to channel these hours into some productive effort.

Oh, of course, there are difficulties, obstacles, distractions. There always have been. Don't delude yourself with the alibi that you need "more time" to put your air castle on a firm foundation. Leisure, you know, can become a debilitating disaster. Let me tell you a true story:

In England, in the year 1775, there was born a young man who had, so far as we are able to discern, absolutely no aptitude for business. Nevertheless, he was compelled by circumstances to spend thirty-three years of his life performing distasteful clerical duties in a London countinghouse. Twelve hours a day he worked, six days a week, the year around. At home the care of a periodically demented older sister took much of his strength, left little leisure.

Yet, somehow, this man—his name, as you may have surmised, was Charles Lamb—found time—*made time*—to create a prodigious quantity of prose and verse, including essays that give him enduring rank among the masters of his craft.

Then, in his forty-ninth year, this mild, busy little man realized the dream of a lifetime. He was retired on an annual pension—given the great gift of *time*. With his sister no longer a burden, he moved to the suburbs to revel in writing. The leisure proved demoralizing. Until he died eight years later—as the result of an accidental fall—Lamb frittered his days away, unable to create a worthwhile line.

Now, it is certain that few of us could become immortal

essayists regardless of how much—or how little—time we had
at our command. But we can do *something*—raise mushrooms,
start a goldfish farm, become an authority on ceramics. In fact I
personally know dissatisfied jobholders who have found relief
and relaxation in these very avocations.

Oh, yes, you have *time*. Even the merest fragments of an odd
hour may be put to constructive use. The late Charles W. Eliot,
long-time president of Harvard University, used to assert that
any literate person could acquire a classical education with an
investment of fifteen minutes a day!

Years ago, before the era of the motorbus, I knew a streetcar
motorman who had a passion for posies. All his life he had
wanted to grow flowers. Unfortunately he lived in a city flat,
with scarcely room for a flower box. But out on the edge of town,
at the end of his run, the streetcar company owned a barren,
unsightly quarter of an acre, used as a turntable. Here, on each
trip, the motorman had a layover of seven minutes. With this
meager allotment of time, amounting to scarcely more than an
hour a day, our motorman cleared, spaded, planted and cultivated that unpromising tract. In a matter of weeks he transformed it into a bower of beauty. In the process he transformed
himself from a disgruntled, dejected workman to an animated,
vitalized person with a consuming personal interest.

This brings to mind the case of another flower enthusiast—a
man who didn't even know he had an interest in growing things
until he developed it quite by accident. He operates a cotton-bag
plant in a Southern city. It is a lucrative but hardly an inspiring
occupation. To employ an active mind he turned to various
hobbies. Then, some ten years ago, a neighbor gave this man a
few scrub camellia bushes. They flourished and flowered. Our
friend's interest grew correspondingly. The next season he bought
some better varieties. Finally he acquired a small greenhouse,
then a larger one. Today he is one of the nation's recognized
camellia experts. The creator of many new varieties, his services

are constantly in demand as a judge at flower shows all over the country. The bag business still yields him a living, but camellias give him a rich and satisfying life.

The story I have just related brings out a point worth noting. Not all of our restless, yearning malcontents are wage earners. Many an individual with a prospering enterprise is vaguely discontented—perhaps because, like an Iowa friend of mine, youthful ambitions were thwarted through some unavoidable circumstance. This Iowan wanted to be an actor—he wound up an undertaker! The fine, long-established family business had to be carried on by someone. As the only son he became, at the sudden death of his father, the unwilling but inevitable nominee.

The would-be thespian used to brood over his fate. However, the last time our paths crossed he looked ten years younger; I have rarely encountered a happier mortician. The solution was simple. Since he couldn't go on the stage, he brought the stage to his town. He launched a local Little Theater movement. It was prospering mightily. And he couldn't have been more elated over a Broadway triumph.

I could go on multiplying instances, but it all comes down to this: If you can't find joy in your job, don't let the situation send you to a psychiatrist. Seek an outlet for your creative urges in a congenial avocation.

XVII THE NEW LEISURE:

A Challenge and a Chance

IT WAS BOB HOPE on a television program who once directed our attention to the possible remote future problem of celebrating six-day weekends with only one workday sandwiched between in which to make a recovery.

While this prospect is admittedly a little on the fantastic side, even to advocates of the long weekend, at the same time we have to begin to think sincerely and soberly of the challenge presented by steadily increasing leisure for a very substantial part of our citizenry.

No civilization of which we have any record has ever had as much leisure as is now promised us—and survived the experiment. One after another they have fallen, victims of the all-too-familiar plague of the *i*'s—indulgence, indifference, incompetence, instability, and finally, infirmity. What assurance have we that we shall make a better showing? Why believe that we have gleaned a secret withheld from others through these thousands of transitional years?

One thing we must come to realize is that the art of leisure must be mastered. Time and leisure are by no means synonymous.

Time is merely a collection of moments until some cherished leisure occupation gives them special meaning.

The essence of leisure is that it must always represent a minor factor in our time calculations. A few precious moments—a few golden hours—husbanded from the day's occupation. The moment we have too much leisure, suddenly we have none at all. The spell is broken. The dream has vanished.

It is for this reason that I have always been among those who are rather dubious of the advantages of the long weekend and the short workweek. As a certain labor leader, reputedly W. W. Reid, put it to his men: "Why do you want the 34-hour week? All it can give you is more time to spend the money you won't have." In other words, leisure will deplete your purse because you can't have leisure without paying out cash somewhere along the line to somebody to entertain you.

If education does not prepare men for unaccustomed leisure, then the world stands in grave danger. "It must be understood," says André Jouve, "that for the great majority of human beings in the present state of their culture, even in the so-called civilized nations, obligatory daily work is a benediction." Man may not relish his job. He may find it highly distasteful. That is his privilege. But it is, nevertheless, his salvation until something else comes along.

That "something else" will not be merely the three-day-a-week vacation tossed into an idle lap. What is man—average, unimaginative man—going to do with all that time? Avocations take time; they are not developed on the spur of the moment. In a recent survey of 92 well-adjusted adult men in New York City, it was found that 68 of that number had begun in their teens developing hobbies which in course became avocations.

How much more leisure do we really want? Perhaps that is the crux of the matter. Never before have so many people spent so much time (and incidentally so much money) having so much fun. How much more can we take?

It has been estimated by the *American Investor* that our people
spend $32 billion a year for recreation. That's nearly 7 per cent
of the total gross national product of goods and services. A
rather staggering sum. We have on an average 1,040 more hours
yearly than our parents had in which to spend recreation money.
Now, supposing our leisure is increased by a third, how are we
going to find the money with which to fill in that added measure
of time? Moreover, if everybody is working less, how can we get
these extra goods to meet our new-leisure allotment?

In addition to every other consideration, what in heaven's
name will we *do* with this great burden of time?

Well, what do we do now? There's photography. Some 60
million of us own cameras. Picture taking is our universal hobby.
But, after all, most of us are just that—picture takers. We have
no deep interest in photography. Who wants to spend much more
time shutter-bugging?

Golf? In the United States some 36 million persons play ten
rounds of golf or more annually on the 330,000 acres of land
regularly maintained for 5,358 golf courses. Suppose *double* that
number should suddenly decide to take up the game. This would
be only a small segment of the new leisure group. Where would
they go? Where *could* they go? The public links are already
crowded. Private courses, generally speaking, have waiting lists.

Travel? Where's the money coming from for these extra jaunts?
And where can you go that the neighbors haven't already stored
up pictures of their previous, and much more de luxe, excursion?

Hunting? Fishing? The trails grow tougher and less rewarding
year by year. And, besides, half the fun lies in *stealing* a few
precious hours from the job.

Yet, despite all these considerations, the four-day workweek
doubtless is on the way, whether too many people really want it
or not. In my active business lifetime I have seen the workday
brought down from twelve hours to eight; the workweek reduced

from six days to five. Why should we assume any change in this trend?

The shorter workweek will come for one paramount reason: Organized labor wants it. They want to set the basic workweek as low as possible, thus presenting the maximum possibilities for overtime. Or, when overtime is not available, an employee may go in for "wildcatting" or taking a second job in a different plant, thus working two full shifts a day.

Well, if the shorter workweek—the longer and more abundant leisure—seems clearly in the cards, what steps can you take to help your child take these hurdles in stride?

The one big thing, probably, is to take a special interest in the youngster's hobbies, helping him to further and cherish those that hold promise of developing into good, healthy avocations for later life. Talk with your child candidly about leisure and the constructive use of it; the importance of developing in a variety of avenues. Impress upon him that decisions must be made well in advance. "I always have something interesting lined up to do before I can find the time to do it," says one healthy-minded teen-ager, who probably will never have vocational problems.

I know a young man—an accountant—who has developed what I think is an ideal approach to the leisure problem. This man is with a firm that expects to go to the four-day workweek within a few years. All signs point to it. And he will be ready. For he has already developed what he calls his "dedicated" day. On Friday morning he will take his briefcase and go forth as usual—but not to the office. He will stop at the office of the local Community Chest where the various agency members can consult with him on accounting problems. In the afternoon he plans to audit records of his luncheon club and in the evening will do a light bookkeeping chore for his bowling league. To those who might consider this young man "a little touched in the head" for his generous gestures (no fees are to be charged in any case) I can only say that he is looking forward to coming Fridays as "the most relaxing day in my week." He is doing something he really likes to do, in a way that he thoroughly enjoys. I, too, can see where it will be a lot of fun.

To others I can only say that you will be amazed at the number of local organizations that will welcome your specialized skills with open arms. And it's a wonderful way to get yourself established in a community. Your child might even begin now by rendering some specialized service to his class. At any rate, it's an idea.

XVIII

CAPITALISM AND COMMUNISM:

The Patchwork Pattern

IN REFLECTING UPON the world your children will inherit we must first consider whether there will be any world a quarter of a century hence. Unhappily this is no longer an academic question. It has become the great reality of our time—a query with which we must deal forthrightly. To individual death we are inured. But the prospect of collective death—the annihilation of the human race—leaves us appalled.

Yet it is a question we must face now—resolutely and realistically—for the sake of our children and succeeding generations.

Let us begin with the common-sense premise that we shall neither convert the Communists nor crush the communistic philosophy. Communism is now too deeply embedded in the minds of too many men. Nor shall we necessarily succumb to this alien philosophy.

Your children will live—if they live at all—in a world dominated by two equally balanced powers, two contrasting philosophies, neither strong enough to overwhelm the other. I

159

think we may put it as bluntly as this: it is either coexistence or no existence.

The age of conquest has at long last come to a dead end. The era of compromise is at hand. We in this troubled hour must lay the foundations for enduring peace. We must effect some realistic limitation of arms. And we must do it right speedily, before the instruments of wholesale destruction become more widespread.

At this moment only America, Russia and Great Britain possess the facilities for nuclear annihilation. If nuclear power spreads to the little countries—the dime-a-dozen dictators—our danger is fantastically enhanced. For then there is always the chance that some petty potentate—some mad messiah—will press the right button at the wrong time and end this long, human saga in the blackest, bleakest night this scarred and weary world has ever known.

Incomprehensible as it may appear to the unthinking, I wish the U.S.S.R. a tolerable measure of progress and prosperity. For in this progress—and in this prosperity—lies our greatest factor of safety. If, with all our rich resources, we cannot accept this challenge—cannot outmatch the Soviet at every turn—then America is indeed suffering from tired blood.

I do not fear an ascendant Russia half so much as I should dread the prospect of a sudden catastrophic collapse of the Communist system. So long as the Soviet is making some progress, showing at least a gradual improvement in living standards, we need fear no precipitate attack. The Russians would have far more to gain by continuing an ordered forward march.

On the other hand, should they observe the walls of their social structure crumbling in threatened collapse, then we must beware. It is when dictators are compelled to drink the bitter dregs of their dreams that reckless, suicidal measures may be employed as a final, desperate resort.

I do not imply that either Communism or capitalism will continue unaltered; that is not the nature of any social or economic system. I confidently expect a very substantial liberalization of the Communist structure. Indeed there are already faint evidences of deviation. The Communisms of Tito's Yugoslavia and Gomulka's Poland differ substantially from the Soviet pattern, although they are, to be sure, very far from being democratic social orders.

This gradual liberalization of the Communist structure is inevitable for a number of reasons. One consideration is the growing importance of the professional class—the scientists, technicians, educators and highly skilled artisans. These people have a stake in stability. They want law and order—increasing material comforts and conveniences—a secure future for themselves and for their children. Theirs is becoming a dominant voice that must in time penetrate and influence the governing realm.

Perhaps without quite realizing the consequences of her action, Russia signed the doom of despotism when she resolved a generation ago to impose universal schooling upon a half-illiterate people. Once you have opened the minds of men you can never again close them to the influences of a wider world. You cannot insulate an educated intellect to the seeping potency of arresting, challenging ideas.

It seems to me significant that the 1956 revolt in Hungary and the more recent restlessness in China were instigated by the younger element—youngsters who grew up under a Communist order. These were not, as some Americans appear to believe, rebellions against Communism, but protests against the restrictive measures of specific dictatorships. Twenty years hence these youths will be in command. They will be running the show. I take this as a heartening portent of things to come.

In a mundane world the essential communal philosophy quickly evaporates; power inevitably gravitates to a small governing group—what Djila terms "The New Class"—who manipulate the total property of the people for their personal aggrandizement and the perpetuating power of the party.

We should not conclude from this obvious weakness that some modification of the Communist philosophy is a wholly impracticable undertaking. Those of you who have traveled, as I have, in the Scandinavian countries must conclude that Socialism, as practiced particularly in Sweden, works remarkably well—for the Swedes.

It is not for us, of course, with our rich heritage of capitalistic freedom. However, I can envision the U.S.S.R. in the next quarter of a century developing a form of government new in our modern world—a government that will take on some of the coloration of Swedish Socialism and American capitalism, without wholly renouncing the foundational philosophy of Marxism.

At this point someone will ask, "How about the atheistic banner?" This, of course, was tacked on inadvertently because Karl Marx—a confused, embittered Jew, baptized as a Protestant—lost his religious convictions and sold the small Bolshevik band a bill of goods.

Atheism is totally alien to the mystic Slavic mind. While it appears rooted in Soviet Communism, we can anticipate that an educated and enlightened governing group will gradually modify restriction against organized religion. I hardly expect your children will live to see Russia officially classified as a "Christian nation," Western type. I do anticipate the complete elimination of religious persecution, perhaps within ten years.

XIX THE AGE OF POWER

WHEN WE SAY that our children will
live in a pattern of steadily expanding power, there is no one
alive today who can accurately express the extent of that power
expansion by, let us say, the end of this century. It is simply
beyond calculation. The ratio is perhaps that of the Wright
brothers' original airplane motor in relation to a modern turbojet.

When atomic power is more fully developed—and when
eventually hydrogen power is added to our treasury—we shall
have the means to bring about miracles that seem too incredible
even for human contemplation. With their forces at our beck we
can quite literally transform our earth into an Eden of our own
choosing, rearranging mountains, rivers, valleys to better suit our
purpose. One relatively small change that perhaps need not await
the full development of our nuclear powers: one of these times,
not too many years away, we shall have roadside illumination
so powerful along our main highways that night driving will
actually become safer than driving by day.

We are still a considerable distance from large-scale applica-
tions of either atomic or hydrogen power. A good guess is that
by 1980 about 10 per cent of the total energy consumption in
the United States will be supplied by nuclear forces. This is an
estimate of the National Planning Association. Whether any

of this power will come from hydrogen sources is highly speculative. It may take us somewhat longer than that to tame this fantastic power.

Without going into technical detail we can say that what the physicists are trying to do is to contain, here on earth, a power plant with the heat intensity of a sun. Whereas the energies of the sun are held in check by the forces of gravity, such playthings are not available to man here on earth. He can make a hydrogen power plant; that is essentially what we have in the hydrogen bomb. However, man cannot get control and draw off the heat thus generated to be converted into electric power.

The only way of solving the problem that has received serious attention thus far is the use of magnetic fields. The electrically charged hot reacting gas is then acted upon by magnetic forces. In other words, these magnetic fields serve as a container for these hot gases. Both the United States and Britain have built experimental machines embracing this principle. To be practical such machines must operate at temperatures of hundreds of millions of degrees. A temperature of possibly five million degrees has been attained by the British, which, it can be readily seen, leaves a long way to go.

Atomic power presents much less formidable problems. We are beginning to feel that we are veterans in this area. We already have atomic power plants in actual operation for civilian use. And more of these will be constructed right along. But, as we have seen, they are not going to make a very big dent in the total energy consumption for a long time to come.

Looking ahead twenty-five years, M. S. Oldacre, an energy consultant, sees us using oil and gas in increasing quantities, but most likely at a decreasing percentage of the total energy supply. Water power will increase an absolute amount, but will become a smaller portion of the total energy supply. Coal and lignite will become much greater factors in the total energy supply. Nuclear energy may be expected to supply a small portion of the total energy needs—possibly 5 to 10 per cent of the electric energy developed in the country. A figure of 5 per cent might be set for 1975; 10 per cent for 1980.

Even if the total of nuclear energy gets up to 10 per cent in 1980—as estimated by both the National Planning Association and private sources, if energy consumption continues to accelerate at anything like the present rate—and it should do infinitely better—this will mean that twenty years hence nuclear energy will be accounting for as much electric power as are all other sources at present. That will make a pretty respectable total.

Probably, however, it will take greater development of atomic and hydrogen power than we now see in the offing to further some of the more elaborate projects that have been proposed. Meanwhile nuclear power is likely to develop somewhat more rapidly in other countries—notably in England, which lacks other fuel resources.

One project tentatively discussed here for years—the reclamation of sea water for domestic use—has already taken a practical turn in Britain, where a test plant is now in operation in Wales. One answer to this is that Britain is hard pressed for water, not only at home but in foreign areas as well. With water conversion a proved success—and power available through nuclear sources —it is highly probable that Britain will move on to Africa, where large areas of desert may be reclaimed. It was long the dream of the British Empire that Africa would one day provide the food for overpopulated and over-industrialized England. Sea water made palatable and nourishing may prove the eventual answer. Only this time it must be the functioning of free enterprise rather than colonial dominance.

You may have been slightly surprised at the forecast of consultant Oldacre, in which he saw coal and lignite becoming much greater factors in the total energy supply. This is understandable when you consider the relative quantities of these materials. Coal and oil are at present producing about equal amounts of power in the world. But the stores of coal are greatly in excess of the oil supply. Dr. George Thomson, the Nobel prize-winning physicist, has estimated that there may be five million million tons of coal reasonably accessible in the earth. Since we are using about 1,300 million tons a year, this would indicate a theoretical supply of coal for four thousand years.

In contrast to this showing, we might estimate oil stores at, say, 10,000 million tons, against an annual consumption of 400 million tons. According to these figures, then, oil reserves could expire within about twenty-five years. There was a time when we were quite worked up about this and there was much talk of alternate fuels. I rather doubt, however, that your children will have occasion to burn motor fuel other than some form or derivative of gasoline. Note that we are now beginning to derive oil direct from shale, of which we have almost limitless stores. This oil will become economically competitive with oil derived in the usual manner.

In a way, perhaps, it is too bad that the "oil scare" didn't last a few years longer. It might have driven us to refine the gasoline motor, which is perhaps the most wasteful and inefficient powerhouse devised in modern times by the hand of presumably ingenious man. In your family car you should be getting at least twice your present mileage from a gallon of gasoline.

XX

LET'S TAKE A LOOK
AT TRANSPORTATION

THERE WILL STILL be railroad passenger trains choo-chooing their way across the country on regularly scheduled runs—perhaps a score of different rail systems—when the twentieth century comes to an end.

This flat statement will come as something of a surprise to many persons who for a decade have been anticipating the demise of rail service.

Certainly this is no effort to tint a pretty grim picture with a rosy hue. The rail situation is bleak, and no denying that. The rail lines lost a billion dollars on their passenger service in 1958; the 1959 figure will be even more depressing. The number of passenger-train employees is at the lowest point it has reached in a century. Out in the yards long-experienced engineers and firemen, now on freight service, bemoan the fact that at the rate trains are being jerked they will never get a passenger run.

Of course the railroads are abandoning trains as rapidly as possible. State officials permitted 1,200 trains to be canceled in the period between 1951 and 1956—and only since that time has the situation become acute. In 1958 the New York Central dropped 10 per cent of its annual passenger train miles (a passenger train mile equals one train traveling one mile).

It is not so much the drop in passenger revenue, it is the accelerating rate that makes rail men dizzy. While the 1956 decline in revenue passenger miles (one paying passenger carried one mile) was only 1.6 per cent below 1955, the 1957 drop was an estimated 20 per cent under 1956, and in 1959 the figures were still basement-bound.

A state may grant permission to abandon trains operating solely within its borders. When interstate traffic is involved, the Interstate Commerce Commission takes over. Thus far most of the trains abandoned represent consolidations or the elimination of costly duplicating services. There are exceptions. Paducah, Kentucky—a city of 65,000—now has no passenger service whatever. The Atchison, Topeka and Santa Fe Railroad no longer runs trains to Atchison, Kansas. (It never did enter Santa Fe, New Mexico.)

Naturally local businessmen fight to hold their trains wherever possible, but on the whole they are playing a losing game. One by one the trains steal away to the boneyard. "Sure, people want to hold their trains," an embittered railroad executive said recently to a *Wall Street Journal* reporter, "they want something to set their clocks by. But they quit riding with us long ago."

No question about it, the trains are being squeezed between the faster planes and the lower-priced buses. Often the handicap is too much to overcome—for example, three days from coast to coast by train as against a between-lunch-and-dinner schedule on a modern jet. Moreover, meals, tips and loss of time considered, the plane may be definitely cheaper.

Yet, despite this discouraging survey, we say there will be passenger trains fifty years hence. Why? There are a number of reasons why we simply cannot afford to do without certain types of trains. For example, the businessman will always need a train that he can board in the late afternoon in one major city and arrive in another—300 to 600 miles away—the next morning. For this type of service the plane is too fast and the bus too slow.

Another consideration is that the government—in the interests of all the people—cannot permit the abandonment of trains to a point where mail delivery would be jeopardized. We sometimes are inclined to forget that much of our mail—except that specifically routed by air—travels by train. There is also our vast cargo of parcel post and railway express. If it were not for trains to move these wares, the confusion would be intolerable. Planes could take only a tiny fraction. Freight service is inadequate and far too slow.

How can the rail lines continue to operate passenger trains if they are out of pocket a billion dollars a year or more? That is a question to which many a railroad now would like an answer. Actually, in the long run, there is only one solution—government intervention in one form or another.

The government must be assured of the continuous operation of the rail lines, not only for the reasons indicated but also because of the matter of national defense.

When you reflect how our rail lines were pressed to absolute capacity during World War II you can see the imperative importance of keeping the service intact and functioning for any national emergency. As a matter of fact, as the rail lines have been retiring coaches and sleeping cars, the armed services have been buying and "stockpiling" this equipment in case of sudden need.

If the government eventually has to take over the rail lines to keep them operating, certainly it will not hesitate to do so. But there are a number of alternative proposals. Perhaps the most intriguing of these suggestions is a plan for the government to buy high-speed passenger equipment as a defense reserve, then make it available to the roads on a lease basis. In this case the roads would be able to operate at maximum efficiency without the heavy investment of capital which they don't have and probably can't raise. In theory at least the government invest-ment—huge though it admittedly would be—could be amortized over a period of years. It looks like one of the more practicable plans now under consideration.

In any case I think you can safely assume that the children of your present preschool-age children will have the "choo-choo" train in their vocabulary.

The future of intracity buses is a bit indefinite. In the long range I look for them to prosper, but they have some trying times ahead. The buses, too, have been losing passenger revenue. Here the chief competitor is the motorist who elects to drive his own car. On a run of any reasonable length the private motorist can make better time than the bus, since he does not have to make so many stops. The motorist has the advantage of controlling his time schedule and also the added asset of having his transporta-tion available at destination.

The bus is much too important a medium to be sold short. For traveling distances of fifty to two hundred miles it has, for many patrons, no serious competition. However, the bus lines are going to have to spruce up a bit, taking a few pointers from European tour operators whose buses often are much more luxurious, and certainly more comfortable, than some of those operating in America. Schedules can be improved and there is a definite need for more and better through service. It can be said with some assurance that the bus is here to stay.

The automobile will continue to be the principal form of personal transportation. However, I do not anticipate that the industry will expand at the rate of the past twenty-five years, unless the export market develops more rapidly than now seems probable. In 1957, for the first time in a peacetime era, New York State actually showed a slight decrease in the number of registered motor vehicles. This was due primarily to a new law barring certain decrepit vehicles from obtaining a license and taking to the highway. It does indicate rather forcefully that the era of unlimited increase is drawing to a close.

To say that we are approaching a stable replacement market for motorcars is an inaccuracy. We still have a growth situation and shall have for the foreseeable future. It is just that the *rate of growth* may be expected to slacken somewhat. We shall have annual increases in population, to be sure, and these will stimulate demand. After all, keep in mind that 75 per cent of American families own automobiles. We cannot hope to go a great deal further than that. Subtracting the subsistence level and those too old or infirm to drive, you haven't much of a market left.

True, only 14 per cent of these families have two or more cars. And that is the real target for our future. Even so, there are a great many households where only one car is desired and many other situations where the second car simply cannot be afforded.

To sum up, then, we can see for the motor industry healthy growth, but hardly fantastic expansion.

I do not see much immediate prospect for the fantastically modern car about which you have been reading of late. My reference is to the so-called "drive-itself" automobile which already has been blueprinted. Cars can be built—and indeed have been built—capable of steering themselves around the traffic hazards without manual aid. The catch to their early adoption is not in the construction of the cars but in the fact that they require a special type of roadbed for their operation. Up to the present no one has contrived a system of electronic control for cars without embedding a low-frequency cable in the highway. This, of course, makes the electronic idea much too costly for widespread use on our highways. However, the problem is under close study and is in the "anything can happen" realm.

This doesn't mean, of course, that electronics aren't going to make some extremely valuable contributions to the future design and construction of cars. Already there is an electronic device that senses faulty co-ordination of the driver. It is so sensitive as un-erringly to refuse to turn on the ignition switch for a drunken driver.

Naturally the cars of the future will look far different from to-day's creations, just as our cars differ radically from those of yesterday. Trying to guess the styles of a quarter of a century ahead is, however, sheer nonsense. No one can have the slightest notion what materials will then be available.

One of the features I rather anticipate in cars of the not-too-distant future is the single control for steering, accelerating and braking. This, in the advance models thus far designed, bears some relation to the airplane "stick." The operation is not unlike that of the old-time electric motorcars. You press forward on a lever, the car starts; the farther you press the greater the accelera-tion. To negotiate a curve you tilt the lever in the direction of the curve. To halt the car, pull backward on the lever.

The combination airplane and automobile is, of course, a reality. Such a vehicle meeting all CAA and highway regulations is in actual production on the West Coast. You can walk into the factory at Longview, Washington, place your order, and pres-ently be the proud possessor of a flying automobile. I do not an-ticipate that this innovation is going to flood the market, but some of your more adventurous youngsters will be driving them ten years hence.

We have read a great deal concerning the "family helicopter," a vehicle promised us at intervals for the past decade. I cannot see the personal airplane (with the possible exception of the flying automobile) doing a great deal to solve our suburban transportation jumble. Airplanes in this situation cost too much money and fly too few persons too short a distance to be eco-nomically rewarding. At best they still require considerable space for take-off and landing, and are generally too cumbersome to get people to the daily job and back again. For this particular chore, I fear that for the foreseeable future we shall be stuck with our private car pools plus suburban trains and buses. Here and there an intrepid individual with the mark of the explorer in his countenance will soar over our rooftops on his way to the country house or the brush factory. But for the most part we just don't have $5,000 to put into a revolutionary craft that carries only two persons. And in addition there are, of course, the heavy —and quite undeterminable—costs of maintenance and operation. You can buy quite a lot of commuter tickets for that kind of money.

Of course, I am not precluding the possibility that someone may come along someday with a completely new form of transportation. You will observe in this book that all along I have been quite chary on the subject of new inventions. I have tried to steer clear of things for which at least preliminary models have not been made. That's because I lack "cornering" vision. I can't see around those corners.

In this respect I recall the classic case of the science writer and the plastic plow handles. We have had plastics, you know, for quite a long time—since the invention of celluloid in 1869, to be precise. This science writer finally got around to doing a piece on the new material, about 1875. By that time it wasn't so new, having been made into a lot of things, including pocket combs, billiard balls and collars and cuffs. Our writer saw considerable possibilities in the stuff and concluded: "I should not be surprise to find seventy-five or a hundred years hence many larger articles . . . such as plow handles . . . made from plastics."

Now, there was a perfectly sound forecast for you. Certainly a case of using the old bean. The surmise was perfectly logical. Only one thing wrong: Our journalist of 1875 couldn't see around corners either. He couldn't know that a generation before 1960 the old family plow would itself be plowed under by the powerful opportunistic tractor—an invention of which no one could possibly have dreamed in that distant day.

XXI THE FARMER IN THE WELL

Food and Our Futur

THOMAS ROBERT MALTHUS,
the English economist, believed that, since population increases faster than the means of subsistence does, in time many must starve or be ill-fed.

The disciples of Malthus would have had a time making a case in America today. In other parts of the world, yes, population *is* getting out of hand. It must be dealt with, and summarily. On the other hand, in the United States, rolling along comfortably with our fifty-three persons to the square mile, we are not concerned. Our population could double and then double again and we would be in no trouble so far as food production is concerned. As seen in an earlier chapter, our population is likely to level off early in the twenty-first century, as Europe's has already done. At that time we probably will have somewhat less than 250 million persons. We may even register slight population losses for a time. But if the opposite proved true and we showed a net increase

175

in the range of 1 per cent, or about two and a half million persons, a year net gain of births over deaths, we should have no difficulty feeding all these new mouths for a very long time to come.

However, any such prodigious birth rate would throw the whole economy out of kilter. We'd go bankrupt trying to provide schools. Living standards would be terribly impaired as fewer and fewer producers sought to provide goods for the rising tide of young unproductives. We might have to revive child labor in self-defense as a final resort. But nothing like this is going to happen, so settle back and relax.

The farm problem is, and has long been in the United States, of quite a different order. For fifteen years we have faced the chronic plight of overproduction, with the government building up larger and yet larger surplus stores. The truth is that we are such a long way from our production peaks that it actually is difficult for us to farm slovenly enough to stay within limitations. If there were any reason at all to expand, doubling our production, even from present peaks, wouldn't present an insuperable problem, with a few years' time and a grant of a few billion dollars. Then we could go on from there. In terms of the European countries, America hasn't begun even to think of straining her productive resources. There has never been any occasion in world history which forced us to do so. Even through two World Wars we hardly noticed the privations.

Consider the case of Holland, with a population density ten times that of the United States. Is there a food shortage? Ask anyone who has visited the Netherlands. The people of Holland live remarkably well and in addition she is one of Europe's largest exporters of dairy products. We don't know anything about that kind of intensive agriculture. We have never had to resort to it. Perhaps we never shall have to do so.

In Europe for uncounted centuries the story has been different. With the possible exception of corn, where we are masters, the

average European country gets at least twice the grain production from an acre of ground that we do. They have to!

So we come back to the point that the real problem is the farmer who keeps producing more bushels, barrels and tons of agricultural commodities than the rest of us can consume. There are just too many farmers, cultivating too many acres and garnering too much from them. What to do?

In the old carriage factory when too many men got to making buggy whips, and inventories rose abnormally, it was a simple matter to put some at making whipstocks; some could paint axles or grease frames. There was no problem.

The farmer is a different breed. Nobody "puts" him at anything. He is an independent operator. When the government limits his acreage, he retires the less productive areas, piles on more fertilizer, and the result is simply bigger crops from less and less land.

Certainly the farmer knows he is outnumbered. There are too many producers to meet the slim appetites of a modern generation. People no longer eat as they used to. And it makes a lot of difference. The farmer realizes this. But he is a farmer. He has always been a farmer. It is the only business he knows. To him farming isn't just an occupation, it is a way of life. He intends to stay right on being a farmer until he is pushed off the farm and into some other occupation.

This pushing process has been going on for a long time now. It catches up with a few hundred here, a few thousand there. Each census shows farm population going down. Eventually the problem will be solved in the only practical way—by the actions of the farmer himself. Gradually but perceptibly he is getting out of the business. It isn't an entirely pretty picture. The old-type family farm is giving way to big-scale mechanized operations. The young men are either going into farming on a real businesslike basis—with enough acreage and enough mechanized equipment to meet the competition—or they are getting out. Most of them, regretfully, are choosing other vocations. Farming just isn't a little man's business any more. Family farms everywhere are being abandoned, merged, reworked. It's the new trend in agriculture. Within a decade it will solve the "farm problem." But it is going to leave a lot of lumps in a lot of throats.

XXII   RACE RELATIONS:

The Tangled Web

ONE OF THE fallacies of the American position is the fixed belief that for every problem there must be an immediate and infallible solution. Some problems are not presently soluble. One of these, in my judgment, is the integration-segregation issue. Oh, it will be settled. The Negro will emerge eventually a first-class citizen of his native land. But here the one essential ingredient is *time*. Any effort to force integration heedlessly and unconditionally on the Deep South will result in incalculable tribulations.

It is popular, of course, to censure the decisions of the Supreme Court; that is an inevitable course of action. Ironically, the decision of Justice Taney in the Dred Scott Case, which aroused the North, was separated by almost precisely a century from the decision sponsored by Justice Warren, which so incensed portions of the South. A great deal depends on the point of view.

Actually, the Supreme Court had no choice. Asked to rule on a point of law it could, in both cases, only come up with an opinion that a law means what it already states. The difficulty lay in the fact that some segments of the country were not ready or willing to have that interpretation read into the law. Their reasons are very real. They are cogent. They deserve respect. But they were not the issue on which the Supreme Court was asked to rule. No one asked, "Is this a wise law?" "Is this a just law?" "Is it a law that is liable to lead to constant bickering and contention?" We asked simply, "What does the law mean?" The court responded with equal simplicity that the law meant what it said. In the circumstances it could hardly have done otherwise.

Finally, then, we go back to the well-meaning friends of integration who are determined to move forward rapidly, regardless of the cost in dislocations. It has been all along the insistence of this group that has brought us to trouble. They are not willing to travel at the pace of the people. Specifically, at the pace of the people in the areas most immediately concerned.

And that pace really is a good deal faster than most persons in other areas realize. Cultured white persons for a generation have known that integration is inevitable. They have been planning for it, working toward it. Their purpose all along has been to elevate the black man a little more in his natural estate, so that when the races meet, as they inevitably must, the racial shock will be less pronounced. A thousand illustrations could be given. Every Southerner has his string of incidents to prove that the Negro is being steadily elevated in the South. If there are not too many disputations and dissensions—"too many LITTLE ROCKS scattered in our path" is the way one trail-blazing peacemaker puts it—most areas of the South could very well be ready for integration in five to ten years. But with continued bitterness and bickering the fuss and furor could string along for half a century.

Primarily there are two reasons that make the Negro a continuing problem in the South. One of these is his very considerable number. That is to say, his number in relation to the white population. The other is his lowly estate.

Obviously the Negro presents no problem in limited numbers. In the small Kansas community in which I was reared there were, I suppose, not more than half a dozen Negro families. To erect a building or hire teachers for so few was unthinkable. Blacks went to school right along with the whites. I recall that the year I was president of my grade school class a Negro girl served as class secretary. No one thought anything of the matter. The young Negroes were neither favored nor fettered by our teacher. They were simply a boy and two girls to be tutored in the elements of arithmetic, geography and English.

Where the Negro outnumbers the white man as he still does in some areas of the Deep South—and where he obviously is of inferior social status—you can understand the apprehension and consternation of those whose living standards are somewhat higher.

"We let the nigger wallow in the slop-trough too long," says one native observer. "Now he comes up and wants to play with us, we're running like scared rabbits. If we had provided him with better schools and homes fifty years ago we wouldn't have this problem now." Of course, we can't go back fifty years and remake the world. We have to do what we can with what we have. And on the whole we are doing a good deal. The plight of the Negro is better—markedly better—year by year.

The notion that the Negro is an especially fecund species is not strongly supported by statistics. He continues to just about hold his own in the percentage of our total population. Of course, like unenlightened persons everywhere, Southern Negroes have tended to have rather large families. But they have been quick to take lessons from the whites. Family size is being adjusted downward in the younger generation. The Negro is not notably long-lived. On the whole, his outlook population-wise would appear to be rather less than average.

As we have seen, the Negro problem in the United States is primarily a matter of geography. And in a degree is being solved geographically. It is being solved in two ways primarily. First, there is the constant movement of Northerners into the rapidly advancing industrial South. This makes for a better balance of whites and blacks. Now, add the steady exodus of the black man from the bayous to the North and the West and you have a double-action force at work. At the rate things are developing, the Negro problem will no longer be a southern problem. To the extent that it continues to be a vexation it can become an *American* problem.

We can handle this matter slowly and sensibly, elevating and integrating the Negro step by step, as rapidly as he can qualify for the status of equality. Or we can rush pell-mell into programs that dramatize immediacy of action—and have bitterness and discord to contend with for the remainder of the twentieth century. The next two or three years are the critical period. They should determine the direction in which we are headed. As a parent you should watch developments with the greatest care. Events that are now shaping up may have a great deal to do with the future course of your child's life. Check on the situation in your own community—even though "race relations" may appear a matter of minor importance in your special area. Seek out the agitators, the troublemakers, those who want to go too far too fast. Learn what is in their minds; what they are thinking, planning, doing. Try, in so far as you are able, to offset their efforts by spreading a philosophy of moderation and thoughtful planning. Join the conservative element in your community. Give it your active support. Let everyone see exactly where you stand. This is a matter of vital importance to your children. Your practical help is sorely needed.

As to what course you should follow in the education of your children: The force of your own example will count far more than all else combined. Practice as well as preach the principles of tolerance based on a genuine belief in the brotherhood of man under the fatherhood of God. But there is no point in being maudlin in our sympathies.

Many Negroes today in various parts of the country must, if they are fair in their judgments, report no race discriminations.

They are enjoying the privileges of first-class citizenship. They hold important posts in government, significant positions in commerce and in the professions. That this number may vastly increase—steadily year by year—is the hope and confident expectation of the moderate group, who work to make this dream a reality. Let us remember that we have been two centuries accumulating the "Negro problem." Let us not hope to solve it in the space of two years.

XXIII   TIME AND SPACE:

The Rugged Race

THIS IS ONE of the more important chapters in our book. It will also be one of the shorter ones. That is because the whole subject of space is so vast it discourages discussion. There is literally no place to start or stop.

A good many people are asking how important space conquest really is. Is it true that he who dominates space can dominate our world as well?

The best answer I can give at the moment seems to be that this is about the size of it. At the same time attention must be called to the fact that space is virtually limitless. So long as two great powers (the man means the United States and Russia) are vying with each other for space control the probabilities are that neither can hope to gain real dominance. It is only if one gives up the struggle or falls seriously behind the other that the remaining contender could hope for a premier position. That is why we call our struggle the rugged race. It is one of those cases where no one cares—or dares—to relinquish a hold. In such a situation the one who holds on could have, quite literally, complete control over the remainder of the world.

How? Why?

There are countless reasons. Consider merely the matter of establishing a small missile-launching base on the moon. Such a venture could soon pay for itself. Because of the lower gravitational pull, a missile would escape from the moon with about one-fifth of the velocity required on earth. This means quicker, easier, cheaper launching. Moreover, missiles could be launched from a side of the moon away from the earth, and yet be controlled from the opposite side. Perhaps the most significant of all effects would be that of deterring an aggressor from a nuclear attack. If A has a Moon base and B has none, the latter certainly will think a long time before planning an attack. Because the moment B strikes, A from his Moon base can bring down complete annihilation upon B and all his kith and kin. And B is not so unperceptive as to lack complete knowledge of that fact.

Another, and by no means minor, phase of this problem is weather control. Dr. Edward Teller, "father of the hydrogen bomb," has pointed out that, should Russia acquire the ability to control weather before we do, she could "dry up" the North American continent simply by bringing in large-scale precipitation in other parts of the world.

All this may appear to be peering a very long way into the future. Nevertheless, the prospect is perhaps not so distant as some of us less aggressive souls might wish. There is now pretty general agreement among scientists that we shall land manned space vehicles on the moon, and probably on Mars. The question of *when* leads to considerably more contention. You can pick yourself almost any date from now until the turn of the century and find a man of science to back up your grabbag selection. The average date for such a landing is set roughly at ten to fifteen years!

Of course, there are a lot of things to be done first. And, at the rate we are going these days, some of these chores could very well be accomplished by the time you read these lines. But the long undertaking—the real stickler—is the round-trip flight.

We know how to get to the moon. Now we have to figure out some way of getting back again. Simple, small-scale models, with animals as passengers, will be under test continuously. Finally, the first man will attempt a journey into space and return. This experiment may be for a limited distance and only after it has been successfully brought off will we consider a trip around the moon—no landing. Eventually, moon landing will be tried but only after several quick round trips.

The successful return of man from a celestial journey will be the biggest news story in human history. This, followed in due course by the landing of man on the moon, will call for piling superlative on top of hyperbole. Sensational and indeed staggering as these events may be, they must be followed by a long, tedious interval before we can hope to put a permanent station of any type on the moon. Nevertheless, it will be the primary topic of scientific discussion as your children grow to maturity. Don't try to discourage your youngster who wants to fare forth in the next space-journeying craft. This is a perfectly natural, healthy ambition for a normal-minded young person growing up in times such as these. It is no more unusual than for yesterday's young man to set his ambition on becoming a motorman. Youth turns naturally to the most glamorous occupation within his ken. Day before yesterday it was operating a streetcar. Tomorrow it will be piloting a space craft. The possibility of such dreams being realized always has been remote. But they serve a useful purpose in the development of his imagination.

As young people grow older they should be encouraged to explore all aspects of the space world. For there it lies, like another America in the days of Columbus. A land of promise to be won through conquest by the courageous. It may not be your child's mission personally to explore this new land—the chances are overwhelmingly against that—but no young person in the years beyond 1960 can live impervious to the rugged race for Time and Space.

XXIV   SOME QUESTIONS
ON THE FUTURE

WHEREVER I HAVE talked to Parent-Teacher groups and other associations on this matter of the child and his future, certain queries have come up during the Question and Answer forum. I have accordingly set down some of these questions, together with my customary responses, in the belief that readers of this book might find the chapter of some interest and value. Perhaps you may have been wanting to ask some of these very questions:

QUESTION: *Will the Russian people revolt?*

ANSWER: No, not in the violent sense in which we use the term. There is virtually no one in active life in Russia today who has personal knowledge of any regime other than Communism. The people have no democratic vision toward which they can march; no recollections on which they can build again.

However, it does seem quite possible that as the Russians give more and more of their people advanced education—thus, in effect, swelling the professional class—it will be necessary to provide somewhat better living and working conditions. It may hardly be necessary for the professional class to make this as a demand. After all, a few years hence, when your children are mature, we shall have a new, younger and presumably more progressive governing group in Russia. They may, without too much badgering, see the wisdom of keeping the nation's most essential group happily and productively occupied.

QUESTION: *How about revolutions in Eastern Europe?*

ANSWER: No; very little chance. And for pretty much the same reasons as in Russia. No core of hard resistance. A generation has now come to maturity under Communism. Pretty hard to get them to act against the only authority they know.

As has been pointed out in another chapter, the Hungarian revolt of 1956 was not primarily against Communism, but against certain specific dictatorial practices. This is a point that has never been well understood in the West.

QUESTION: *Our children, generally speaking, are larger and heavier than their parents. Will their children continue this trend?*

ANSWER: They will continue the trend, but the distinctions may not be so great. We are now breeding our first generation reared on abundant orange juice and cod-liver oil. The result should be fine, healthy offspring. But, after all, you cannot compound these dietary benefits. You merely pass them on to the next generation. Thus acceleration in size and weight may be somewhat slower henceforth.

Moreover, there is some indication that we are approaching our maximal limits anyway. The person who materially exceeds six feet and 225 pounds can become something of a nuisance in the modern world. There is a question whether we want too many of them anyway.

QUESTION: *Should automation be viewed as a threat to the jobs and security of our young people?*

ANSWER: On the contrary. You should bless and cherish every particle of automation American industry is able to put into operation in the next ten or fifteen years. When the canning factory installs more automatic machinery, instead of viewing this as a threat to friends and neighbors, give three cheers. For by this action they are releasing workers for service where they will be even more sorely needed.

Automation is the best insurance your children can have of maintaining high standards of living in the coming years. More people in our nation will require the production of more goods, just to give each his present prorata share. When these population increases are concentrated so heavily in the nonproductive over- and under-age groups, the burden on producers grows heavier. That's where and why automation is needed. Without this aid everyone's standard of living would necessarily fall a notch or two or three simply because there wouldn't be goods enough to go round.

We shall win this tussle. For America has never yet lost a significant production battle. But we shall need those automatic machines. And don't forget it!

QUESTION: *Will women become more dominant in the next generation?*

ANSWER: Dominance is a matter of individuality rather than sex. We have always had dominant women in our society. However, only in the past fifty years have women had full opportunity to display their aggressive characteristics. That they will become more dominant in future seems to me improbable. Most of the victories have been won. There isn't a great deal left over which to be contentious.

Of course, the very smartest women always have known that they could exert their greatest power by yielding strategically. This it seems likely they will continue to do in the battle of the sexes, which actually is rather benign as battles go. Neither side really wants to win and both are triggered for quick surrender.

QUESTION: *Will the nations of Europe stand more closely together in the future, for their economic and social safety?*

ANSWER: On the whole, yes; but with certain definite reservations. Such developments as the "free Europe" common trade market, in which the various states let down their trade barriers

for the common good—and for the solidarity of Europe as a
marketer abroad—is a wholesome portent.

We must remember that the partisan spirit burns fiercely in
Europe. The Frenchman and the West German may work closely
together in trade. Yet each preserves his personal identity and
his patriotism. Each has certain pronounced national characteristics. The Frenchman bubbles and boils while the German
simmers and steams. The German wants someone to take over
and solve his problems. (That is how Hitler got into the saddle
originally.) The Frenchman accepts authority only as a last
resort. And stability of government is not a notable French
achievement.

The Englishman is quite dissimilar to either of his neighbors.
He probably is the most law-abiding citizen in the world. This
is not, as many believe, a trait of weakness. It is just that, having
set up laws in an orderly manner, the Englishman assumes they
are to be obeyed. If the laws are displeasing to a sufficient number, they may seek to have them altered. But so long as a law
remains on the statute books it is to be observed.

Stopping at the Grosvenor House in London once I was
intrigued by a cravat displayed in one of the small specialty
shops. It featured the hotel crest in gold against a navy background. I decided to step in and buy one as a souvenir. The
transaction concluded, I reminded the tradesman that he had
not asked for any evidence of my identity as a guest. The ties
were reserved for guests only.

"Someone," I suggested, "might drop in here from a side-street
hotel and buy one of these emblems."

If I had suggested to the clerk that he knock off work a little
early so as to have time to murder his dear old grandmother
before tea, he could hardly have been more startled.

"Why, sir," he said gravely, "no one would do a thing like
that."

And, do you know, he was perfectly right. No Englishman

would ever think of such a thing. For a nonguest to wear a Grosvenor House cravat would be as unthinkable as to don an old school tie without the correct credentials. That sort of thing simply isn't done.

QUESTION: *What about the "working grandmothers"? What would happen to the economy if any considerable number of them should decide to quit work?*

ANSWER: Women between the ages of 45 and 65 represent about 30 per cent of our female work force. They do not by any means turn out 30 per cent of the work.

Naturally there are plenty of exceptions, but as a group these are part-time workers. Often they work with a definite objective in view. They take a job to acquire a new coat, a refrigerator, or perhaps to pay off some family obligation. When the goal has been attained, they quit. Some are seasonal workers by nature. I know one sixty-year-old matron who labors faithfully all winter, but throws up her job with a whoop of joy on the first warm day of spring.

As to what would happen if these workers struck. That is a relatively simple matter according to orthodox theory. The economy simply becomes poorer by the extent of that person's contribution. We'd have to reduce our standard of living proportionately, since there would be fewer goods and services available. However, this theory is a little too pat and precise to apply to part-time workers. When one quits, the group has a tendency to speed up and absorb the "lost" production. While the departed worker loses in wages, those who remain gain through increased remuneration. The total economy is little changed.

Perhaps the greatest single class of sufferers in such a cessation of labor would be pampered grandchildren.

QUESTION: *Do you see in the future a further reduction in the art of reading?*

ANSWER: What art of reading?

As a nation we appear to be about as far removed from serious reading—aside from clamorous assignments—as we can very well get. The last time I had occasion to check, we were seventh on the list of "civilized" nations in the number of books read per capita. I doubt that we have made much of an ascent in the interval. We may as well face it. Whatever collective virtues we may possess, we are not, as a group, a "reading people." I see no hopeful reason to assume that your children will read even as many books per year as you now scan. That isn't an especially hopeful prospect, is it?

QUESTION: *What is the future of the taxpayer in our modern world?*

ANSWER: This is perhaps the most futile of all queries. No one really needs to ask the question. And no one wants an accurate answer.

Since the cost of government—local, state and national—is getting higher all the time; and since these bills must somehow, at some time be paid, the taxpayer is elected burden-bearer without a single dissenting voice. This tax load is the biggest single burden your child has to face in a lifetime of struggle. At the moment there seems no possible escape. Even though we didn't add a single dollar to the bill—a highly dubious speculation—our children would be kept humping for a natural lifetime just to meet the interest payments on the money we owe.

QUESTION: *If, as you say, people are going to stop smoking, what new habit are they likely to adopt?*

ANSWER: I didn't say people are going to stop smoking. I said *cigarette* smoking is likely to *diminish.* You may recall I gave the habit a good, long fifty-year lease on life before we arrive at a point where the cigarette smoker in our social order is as conspicuous as the nonsmoker now is.

On the whole, I think that whatever habit succeeds cigarette smoking is likely to involve the ingestion of some form of tobacco. From where we stand at the moment the little cigar looks like a possible contender. It is not, of course, a new contender. Several efforts have been made to popularize small cigars but they have never gotten much of a hold on the market. Now, however, things are beginning to look brighter. The industry made 4.3 million little cigars in January, 1958, and over 80 million in January, 1959. That percentage of sales increase doesn't get overlooked.

Actually "little cigars" are of two types and there is as yet no clear public preference. The first is a true cigar of diminutive size. The other is a cigarette-sized tobacco tube filled with cigar tobacco. It is made on a cigarette machine. It tastes and smokes quite different from a cigarette—or a cigar, for that matter.

As yet I have noted no studies on cigarillo, or little cigar, smoking in relation to lung cancer.

I may mention parenthetically that a vegetable-product cigarette has lately been placed on the market. It is said to taste like a regular cigarette, but contains no tobacco.

QUESTION: *Why do you oppose teaching the Christian religion to the people of backward lands, as we have trade relations with them?*

ANSWER: I oppose it because I think it is confusing and defeating to try to sell too many ideas at once. Our business people should stick to their own ideas, buying and selling on a straight commercial basis. I don't think it is wise to expect your star salesman to use the Testament as a sales manual. Let him reflect credit on Christianity in his personal conduct, but not go beyond that point.

Then bring in the experts—the missionaries. Let them set up their schools, churches, hospitals, clinics. That is the way, and the only way, Christians are made—through Christian service. We need not worry too much about "selling" Christianity. People will buy it if the product is right.

QUESTION: *You say our national agricultural resources could feed many more people. How much population do you think we could actually sustain?*

ANSWER: Oh, as far as feeding the people is concerned we could take care of up to 500 million without too seriously disrupting the system. We have the potential resources to feed a billion persons, as far as that goes. But the real pinch would come in other areas of the economy—trying to provide houses, schools and clothing.

You see, in such a rapidly growing population structure more and more of the total population would have to be younger and younger. The adults simply couldn't stand the strain of taking care of so many babes. If we should gain, say, half a billion in two or three hundred years, that should work out without too much disruption. Present indications are that we are more likely to go in an opposite direction.

QUESTION: *Do you feel that we and our British cousins are likely to grow closer together in our language and modes of expression as our communications improve?*

ANSWER: Yes, I suppose so, and I rather dislike the prospect. I think that regional differences in people enrich personalities and add piquant interest to our associations.

Whenever people are isolated from their fellows for a considerable time regional expressions are likely to abound. Up to perhaps twenty-five years ago, in the mountains of North Carolina and Tennessee, you could hear hillbillies using very acceptable Elizabethan English. They had taken it into the mountains with them and passed the expressions (such as "et" for "ate") down for generations.

The converse is of course true. The more we see and hear of each other the more alike we tend to become. It is a little depressing, isn't it?

QUESTION: *In your mention of transportation modes and methods you made no mention of the electric car. Do you think it has a future?*

ANSWER: No great future perhaps. But it has a very pleasant present. A good many small electric cars are beginning to appear around the country, on golf courses, etc. They are ideal for sub-urban shopping. Actually a small electric weighing about 350 pounds should be built for a good deal less than $1,000. Such a car should run 50 miles a day on one charge, and be recharged in the garage each night. Electricity shouldn't run over $3 a month. Top speed: about 30 miles an hour.

Thomas A. Edison was a little touched on the subject of electric automobiles. He made his executives drive electrics around the Oranges many years after others had discarded the vehicle. He once told me that if an effort comparable to that expended on gasoline motors had been put on the electric, that car would have emerged in premier position. We may make some allowances for Mr. Edison's enthusiasms, but there is still a great deal to be said for the electric. I'd rather like to have one myself.

QUESTION: *Do you think as high a percentage of persons in the future will own their homes as presently do?*

ANSWER: On the whole, I see no reason for a diminution of the trend. Of course, there always are persons in transient vocations for whom home-owning is a luxury, and often quite impracticable. But the average householder probably will continue to want to own his home and the loan entrepreneurs surely are making it simple enough for him to do so.

Some young GIs who hastened to buy flimsy shoe-box structures at war's end are liable to be pretty bitter for a time. Many will return to city apartment life. Eventually the urge to try again will have its way.

Yes, I think there will be as many homeowners tomorrow as there are today.

QUESTION: *Do you anticipate that we'll continue our drives for charity organizations in the future pretty much as we now do?*

ANSWER: Perhaps you hadn't noticed, but "charity" drives are now pretty much a thing of the past. The big drives are all for funds for scientific research and developments, not for the relief of the indigent. The Community Chest is no longer a confused group of agencies rendering transient relief to the poor and helpless. These cases are now handled by local, state and national governmental agencies. Your money contributed to the Chest goes chiefly to such character-building groups as the Boy Scouts, the Girl Scouts, Y.M.C.A., Y.W.C.A., etc.

Yes, I think these drives will continue pretty much as in the past. There appears to be no other practicable way for the individual agencies to survive and prosper.

I anticipate that senior citizens with time on their hands will be willing to work as volunteers in certain of these groups where their services are sorely needed as solicitors or as administrators. Also it would be fine if some of our younger groups from the mills and factories—with a little new leisure—would invest a portion of their time in this fine work. Anyone with a sincere wish to serve will be warmly welcomed.

QUESTION: *Do you anticipate any marked change in our system of electing public officials?*

ANSWER: No; the American elective system is pretty well set forth in the Constitution. It appears to suit most of us moderately well. Of course, we don't like some of the individuals who eventually are voted into office under this system. We grumble about them. However, we always have the freedom to vote in a new group we shan't like any better—and we quite frequently do just that.

QUESTION: *Will money continue to be a big factor in the United States or will we use more and more of its symbols, such as credit, etc.?*

ANSWER: Credit in all forms certainly is on the rise, and it sometimes seems that money is becoming old-fashioned. But, no; money—the actual cold cash—still is the foundation of our financial system. We still need a good deal of it. Despite all your charge accounts, credit cards and other gimmicks, consider how much actual cash passes through your fingers in the course of a week. And you always have to keep a little money on hand to pay the paper boy!

QUESTION: *Will the next generation differ materially in appearance and deportment from our present group?*

ANSWER: See the Family Portrait Album, circa 1930.

XXV THE OTHER HALF
OF THE CENTURY

SOME YEARS AGO a scientist connected with the British Museum gained considerable notoriety in his experiments with small animals which he put into deep-freeze, took out, and revived at intervals. The speculation arose as to whether or not the experiment could be extended to the human family.

Let us assume, then, just for the sake of illustration, that a man in the prime of life had been put into deep-freeze in the year 1900, and brought to revival in 1950. It is my opinion that this man would find more of bewilderment and confusion—more to amaze and amuse—than would the individual put on ice today and revived in the year 2000. Naturally there is no warrant for this supposition. It can be only a personal opinion. But it has seemed to me that the first fifty years of this century presented a period of "beginnings" such as the world may never see again. Let me illustrate my point in this way:

The latest turbojet cruiser is but an improvisation on the Kitty Hawk Kite. A hundred times larger and many thousands of times more powerful, it still represents only a series of evolutionary steps. There is no drama in evolution; only in revolution.

Back in 1904 there was nothing. Nothing but a dream. The air belonged to the birds. Then suddenly we looked up and there were the Wright brothers flying around. That was drama. It was wonderful. Wonderful in the literal, venerable sense of being full of wonder.

The same thing holds true as we go right down the list. The automobile, electric light, telephone—all were developed from embryonic beginnings and chiefly in our half of the century. It makes a difference. A mature individual today who can remember when movies didn't talk, when radio and television were in their infancy, can never take quite the same attitude toward these wonders as does the person who has never known anything different.

Don't chide your child for this attitude of seeming indifference or unconcerned acceptance of new wonders as they come along. He is not to blame for the fact that you brought him into the world a generation behind the pioneers.

This indifference is something of a mark in any case. If your child is not particularly surprised at a new invention, it may well be because he has been anticipating it for some time anyway. Children today are amazingly alert and alive; in their perception they have journeyed far beyond the young people of the preceding generation. Even children who are not especially mechanically minded are likely to surprise you with their knowledge of what makes things tick. They know how to take the world's gadgets apart and put them together again. And because they do understand the principles they are not especially surprised at the results.

Perhaps it is too bad that there is no longer much wonder left in the world. That is, after all, the product of an abecedarian culture in which the people are naïve and the materials new. Fifty years ago man and his animals ruled and ran the earth. Its progress was pretty well limited to their productive power. There were a few steam plants; and a little electric power in spots;

here and there some development of water power. Once in a
while you encountered a noisy puffing gasoline motor. Still by
and large the power was produced by man and his animals. Only
since World War I has there emerged a power-freed generation;
a generation able to exercise mind rather than muscle.

To indicate that the creative age is over, that there are no
achievements on the way is, of course, the height of absurdity.
For future developments will far exceed the present.

But they will be built on what has gone before—patterned on
the past, so to speak. After all, you have to move on from where
you came to whither you are destined. You can't keep going back
to Genesis. You have to move on toward Revelation.

Perhaps, naturally enough, those of us who have lived through
Genesis find it difficult to renounce our recollections completely.
We can "remember when" and we like on occasion to do it. We
should be careful not to let this pattern of the past impair our
vision of things to come. "I am interested in the future," said
inventor Charles F. Kettering, "because that is where I expect to
spend the rest of my life." And that's where he did spend it, too,
almost to his final hour.

If your parents attended the St. Louis Exposition in 1904 they
may possibly have encountered Professor Worwordo, an im-
maculately dressed little fellow who, I presume, operated some
sort of back-street concession. My knowledge of the gentleman is
limited to a small souvenir pamphlet I once ran across in a used-
book store. In this small book the professor had undertaken to
present his ideas of the wonders that would unfold during the
course of the twentieth century. A more weird collection of illustrations I have rarely seen. Virtually none of these miracles
ever came to realization, and I think it highly improbable that
any now will. This illustrates the sort of thing that continually
intrigues our minds. In our search for the bizarre and sensational
we overlook the perfectly obvious. Within a few hundred yards
of the professor's little stand there was a building of domestic

science exhibits where a proud manufacturer displayed an early model of the hand-powered vacuum cleaner. Since gasoline and electric motors were no novelty at the time, why didn't it occur to Professor Worwordo—or indeed to the manufacturer—to attach a small motor to that cleaner and thus eliminate the drudgery of hand-pumping? Yes, we always overlook the obvious.

And so I shall make no effort to picture the world of A.D. 2000. My vision is no clearer than yours and I have a feeling that both may be pretty well on the hazy side. I'd be sure to overlook something quite as obvious as the electric-powered vacuum cleaner.

Your children, probably too young even to remember the introduction of atomic and hydrogen powers, will live to see these powers developed to a point where to employ the strength of a thousand horses may mean no more than the mere lifting of a hand.

Naturally, you will encourage your children to live fully and productively in this world of which they are a part. Remember, it is the only world they'll ever know. At the same time you should avoid clinging in the shadows of the past. That is a vanished era. Try as best you can to enter into the world of your children. And if they sometimes seem to take the contemporary wonders too calmly, it probably is because they are better informed on the new enterprises. Likely as not they have been sitting around waiting impatiently for someone to invent that very thing. That is what is likely to happen when you turn your youngsters loose with a challenging problem and the tools and facilities to solve it.

You'll never be able to keep up with your brood as they adventure along through the "other half" of our twentieth century. But at any rate try not to look too "beat up" when, now and then, you get within hailing distance.

XXVI   PERSONAL TO PARENTS

IF, A GENERATION ago, your parents could have foreseen the world in which you live today they would have been panic-stricken: mad vehicles coursing through the air, crossing an ocean in four hours, a continent in the time between lunch and dinner; automobiles racing along highways at 75 or 100 miles per hour; traffic jams; cloverleaf intersections; suburban complications; the vanishing domestic servant; the constant hurry and flurry of getting from Here to There. Yes, all those tribulations added up make quite a stack. But you aren't especially weighed down by them. In fact, you are bearing up remarkably well. And that, of course, is because this change did not come upon you all of a sudden. As the noises and confusion grew, your ability to combat them also increased. So it will be with your own children and the world of twenty-five or thirty years hence.

I regret to have to tell you that your children will face a disproportionately heavier tax burden. This probably will not come as a complete surprise. You have watched your own taxes creep steadily upward through the years. This is a trend of long duration.

The late Justice Oliver Wendell Holmes once observed that

taxes are the price we pay for a civilized social order. If this be the case, then certainly we are getting awfully civilized.

Rising taxes, of course, reflect the growing complexity of our governmental structure at every level—township, city, county, state and federal. More and more people are getting on the payrolls, and it is requiring increasingly huge sums to keep them there. It now costs more to provide paper towels for federal employees than the total government budget of 1908.

Along with higher taxes will come, I strongly suspect, a greater degree of government regulation. For that, too, has been a longtime trend. So we may assume that your children, in their adult years, will lead an even more regimented life than the present generation.

This may seem an appalling prospect. Nevertheless, like your contemporary world of clatter and confusion, of which I spoke a moment ago, it will develop gradually. Your children will adjust to their world just as you have adjusted to developments that your parents would have hailed with terror.

The strongest force you must combat, in all probability, is the urge to live your child's life. Don't succumb to this persistent temptation. There is room in every life for the full expression of only one personality. It should by every right and justice be the personality that is born with that life. Don't take advantage of your child's natural inclination toward parental discipline to foist your ideas, prejudices, convictions and aspirations onto a pair of amenable young shoulders. You have lived your life. Let your child have a chance at his.

Now, as a final admonition: Don't worry too much about this younger generation. After all, the world in which they live will be *their* world. They will have made it. And they will get along all right in it. They have a great heritage back of them.

Remember—*they are your kids!*

Set in Baskerville by Brown Bros. Linotypers, Inc.
Format by Dorothy M. Hagen
Manufactured by The Haddon Craftsmen, Inc.
Published by Harper & Brothers, New York